Decisiveness of Israeli Small-Unit Leadership on the Golan Heights in the 1973 Yom Kippur War

Oakland McCulloch

THE DECISIVENESS OF ISRAELI SMALL-UNIT LEADERSHIP
ON THE GOLAN HEIGHTS IN THE 1973 YOM KIPPUR WAR

A thesis presented to the Faculty of the U.S. Army
Command and General Staff College in partial
fulfillment of the requirements for the
degree

MASTER OF MILITARY ART AND SCIENCE

by

OAKLAND McCULLOCH, MAJ, USA
B.S., Northern Illinois University, DeKalb, Illinois, 1987

Fort Leavenworth, Kansas
2003

Approved for public release; distribution is unlimited.

MASTER OF MILITARY ART AND SCIENCE

THESIS APPROVAL PAGE

Name of Candidate: MAJ Oakland McCulloch

Thesis Title: The Decisiveness of Israeli Small-Unit Leadership on the Golan Heights in the 1973 Yom Kippur War

Approved by:

_____, Thesis Committee Chairman
George W. Gawrych, Ph.D.

_____, Member
COL Lawyn C. Edwards, M.S.

_____, Member
LTC William L. Greenberg, M.M.A.S.

Accepted this 6th day of June 2003 by:

_____, Director, Graduate Degree Programs
Philip J. Brookes, Ph.D.

The opinions and conclusions expressed herein are those of the student author and do not necessarily represent the views of the U.S. Army Command and General Staff College or any other governmental agency. (References to this study should include the foregoing statement.)

ABSTRACT

THE DECISIVENESS OF ISRAELI SMALL-UNIT LEADERSHIP ON THE GOLAN HEIGHTS IN THE 1973 YOM KIPPUR WAR, by MAJ Oakland McCulloch, 118 pages.

This study is an analysis of the decisiveness of Israeli small-unit leadership on the Golan Heights during the 1973 Yom Kippur War. What allowed the Israeli brigades on the Golan Heights to defeat an Arab coalition that launched a surprise attack with a force that vastly outnumbered the Israelis in men, tanks and artillery? The one advantage the Israelis had was the quality of leadership at the small-unit level. This study begins with a brief review of the strategic and operational situation in the Middle East in 1973. This includes background information on the Israeli and Arab forces facing each other on the Golan Heights and their plans for the defense and attack respectfully prior to the start of hostilities. The majority of the thesis discussion is concerned with the actual battle on the Golan Heights. It highlights the contributions that small-unit leadership made during the battle that allowed the vastly outnumbered IDF to destroy a massive Soviet-style Arab army. This portion of the study also looks at the experiences of those Israeli leaders involved in the fighting. The study then looks at leadership from the Israeli perspective. I define what leadership is and why it is important at the small-unit level. I take a close look at how the Israeli Defense Force (IDF) picks and trains its leaders and what role the Israeli Military Culture plays in that process. The conclusion of the thesis is that the IDF was able to fight and win even though surprised and vastly outnumbered due to the quality of leadership at the small-unit level. This lesson may prove to be important still today as the armies of the Western societies continue to get smaller even though they still face the threat of fighting the massive Soviet-style armies of the "Axis of Evil" for decades to come.

ACKNOWLEDGMENTS

I wish to express my deep gratitude to my committee members (Dr. George W. Gawrych, Colonel Lawyn Edwards and Lieutenant Colonel William L. Greenberg) who spent countless hours reading my drafts and mentoring me throughout this process. They continued to push me to not only complete this thesis, but to get it right. I would be remiss if I did not thank my loving family. They endured many hours of me sitting at my computer doing research and writing when they would much rather I be spending time with them. A special thanks to my wife who not only endured reading through my drafts but who went to bed many nights by herself while I typed away on the computer until the early morning. I could not have completed this thesis without the help and support of these people.

TABLE OF CONTENTS

Page

THESIS APPROVAL PAGE ii
ABSTRACT iii
ACKNOWLEDGMENTS iv
ILLUSTRATIONS vi
TABLES ....**Error! Bookmark not defined.**
CHAPTER 1. INTRODUCTION 1
   Background 2
   Arab and Israeli Defenses Along the Golan Heights Prior to the War 3
   The Syrian Offensive Plan 5
   Syrian and Israeli Forces on the Eve of War 7
   The Final Preparations For War 9
CHAPTER 2. THE BATTLE FOR THE GOLAN HEIGHTS 19
   The Battle is Joined--Day 1 19
   Reorganization of the Forces on the Golan Heights 30
   Stubborn Defense in the North and Breakthrough in the South 34
   The Seventh of October--A Near Run Thing 41
   The Initiative Starts to Shift 48
   The Ninth and Tenth of October--Back to the Purple Line 53
CHAPTER 3. ISRAELI LEADERSHIP 66
   Leadership Defined and Israeli Doctrine 66
   Principles of Israeli Small-Unit Leadership 71
   Israeli Leadership Principles Put to Use at the Small-Unit Level 77
   How The IDF Selects and Trains Its Leaders 80
CHAPTER 4. CONCLUSION 88
   Relevance to the U.S. Army 89
   Final Thought 91
APPENDIX A. ISRAELI BATTLE UNITS AND COMMANDERS 93
APPENDIX B. SYRIAN BATTLE UNITS AND COMMANDERS 94
APPENDIX C. ILLUSTRATIONS 95
APPENDIX D. ISRAELI OFFICER'S OATH OF OFFICE 102
APPENDIX E. ISRAELI AND SYRIAN TANK AND
                    ARMORED FIGHTING VEHICLE SPECIFICATIONS 103
BIBLIOGRAPHY 107
INITIAL DISTRIBUTION LIST 110
CERTIFICATION FOR MMAS DISTRIBUTION STATEMENT 111

ILLUSTRATIONS

Figure	Page
1. Map of the Golan Heights with the Relief of the Golan Heights	96
2. Map of Key Locations on the Golan Heights	97
3. Map of the Golan Heights Deployments on 6 October 1973 at 1400 Hours	98
4. Map of the Deployment of Forces on 7 October 1973 at 1400 Hours	99
5. Map of the Maximum Syrian Penetration on 7 October 1973 at 2400 Hours	100
6. Map of Israeli Counterattacks Reaching the Purple Line on 10 October 1973	101

CHAPTER 1

INTRODUCTION

In 1948 the United Nations created the State of Israel in what was British occupied Palestine. Since the first day of Israel's existence the Arab nations of the world have been attempting to destroy the state of Israel by any means available, including the use of force. The Israeli Defense Force (IDF) was born in battle and has been forced to fight repeatedly since Israel's creation: a War of Independence in 1948, the Sinai-Suez War in 1956, the Six Day War in 1967, the Yom Kippur War in 1973 and the War in Lebanon in 1982. The coalition of Arab forces vastly outnumbered the IDF in manpower, tanks, artillery and aircraft and had the advantage of choosing when the war would start, except in 1956 and 1982. With all of these advantages then why is it that the IDF has been so successful in battle against the armies of the Arab coalitions? The quality of leadership at the small-unit level is the one advantage the IDF has had in every war they have fought against the armies of their Arab neighbors.

The purpose of this thesis is to examine the decisiveness of Israeli small-unit leadership in the battle for the Golan Heights during the 1973 Yom Kippur War. To do this I will look at Israeli leadership in several different ways. First, I will define what leadership is and show why it is important to an army, especially one that is numerically inferior to its opponent. Secondly, I will show that Israeli small-unit leadership is decisive due to the way the IDF picks and trains its small-unit leaders. Thirdly, I will show how the competent and confident actions of Israeli small-unit leaders were the decisive aspects of the battle for the Golan Heights during the 1973 Yom Kippur War.

Background

The Arab-Israeli War of 1973 was a war between Israel on one side and an Arab coalition led by Egypt and Syria on the other side. It was the fourth major military confrontation between Israel and the Arab states since 1948 and is also known as the Yom Kippur or Ramadan War.

There were two major factors leading up to the Yom Kippur War. First, there was a failure to resolve territorial disputes arising from the Arab-Israeli War of 1967. These disputes revolved around the Arab nations' demand for Israel to return the Sinai to Egypt, the West Bank to Jordan and the Golan Heights to Syria. Egyptian President Anwar Sadat continued to call for the Israelis to comply with United Nations Resolution 242 since assuming power in September 1970. UNR 242 called for Israel to return all the land it conquered and occupied during the 1967 Arab-Israeli War in return for recognition of Israel's right to exist by here Arab neighbors. However, President Sadat's land for peace initiative failed to bring peace to the Middle East. Sadat wanted to sign an agreement with Israel provided the Israelis returned all the occupied territories, but Israel refused to withdraw to the pre-1967 armistice lines.[1] Since no progress was being made toward peace, Sadat was convinced that in order to force the Israelis back to the negotiating table and to gain legitimacy at home, he must renew the war against Israel.

The second factor leading up to the war in 1973 was the belief by both the Israeli military, at all levels, and the Israeli government that Israel was safe from Arab attack for the indefinite future. Therefore, Israel did not feel compelled to trade territory for peace. Israel felt this way because of the Israel Defense Force's strength, the apparent political disarray of the Arab world, the dismal performance of the Arab coalition during the Six

Day War, and the large buffer zone around Israel formed by the Sinai, the West Bank, and the Golan Heights.[2] Thus, in spite of Sadat's threats of war throughout 1972 and much of 1973, Israeli commanders were unprepared for Egypt and Syria's surprise attack on 6 October 1973.

Arab and Israeli Defenses Along the Golan Heights Prior to the War

The Golan Heights is an escarpment rising 800 to 1,000 meters above the Sea of Galilee and the Jordan Valley. Covering an area some 900 square kilometers (65 kilometers from north to south and 30 kilometers wide at its widest point), the escarpment rises gradually from south to north. These ancient hills were created by volcanic activity; lava pouring out of craters covered the high plateau with layers of basalt. A maze of ridges and wall-like lava patterns, completely impassable even to modern cross-country armored vehicles due to the slopes exceeding 45 degrees, covers most of the northeastern area. Further south the area becomes more open allowing better movement by armored vehicles. Scores of extinct volcanoes rise above the surrounding terrain making excellent vantage and observation points.[3]

In the six years since the end of the Six Day War, the Syrians had constructed three major defensive systems echeloned in depth from the Golan Heights towards Damascus. The first defensive system was sited close to the Purple Line, the United Nations cease fire line between the Israeli Army on the Golan Heights and Syrian Army in the valley below; the second defensive system lay east of the volcanic fields along the Kuneitra-Damascus road; and the third defensive system stood just to the west of Damascus in the Damascus basin. The Syrians manned these defensive systems with anywhere between a brigade and a division depending upon the time of year, and the tension level between Syria and the Israel.[4]

The Israeli defensive concept on the Golan Heights was to delay the Syrian attack long enough to allow strong Israeli reserves time to mobilize and reinforce the regular units. To accomplish this task the Israeli defense was developed based on two principles. The first principle was centered on terrain because the Israelis retained superior positions on the Golan Heights based on well-chosen defensive lines. The second principle was based on the Syrian's doctrine in the attack, which called for the use of massed formations of tanks, just like the prevailing Soviet operational doctrine. The terrain on the Golan Heights is very restrictive and allows the movement of massed tank formations only in a few locations.[5] The Israelis could read the terrain the same as the Syrians and built their defensive fortifications over watching these critical pieces of terrain. This allowed the Israelis to mass their limited forces on the decisive terrain.

During the period of occupation in the six years since the end of the Six Day War, the IDF had fortified the Golan Heights by constructing a system of obstacles and fortifications on the eastern edge of the plateau. The IDF constructed an antitank ditch four to six meters wide and about four meters deep along the entire length and just west of the Purple Line. A system of concrete observation posts and strong points were built just behind the antitank ditch. There were seventeen such fortified positions, with 112 separate fortified and mutually supportive pillboxes and blockhouses. These positions ensured the Israelis would have continuous observation over all of the approaches to the Golan Heights from the east. In front of and behind the antitank ditch was an integrated minefield system around each strongpoint and on the important avenues of approach.[6]

Israeli fortifications and defenses on the Golan Heights were formidable when fully manned with the proper number of infantry and tanks, however this was not the case in October 1973.

In September 1973 the Israelis manned the Purple Line with elements of two infantry brigades, which totaled less than the equivalent of one brigade in strength, and one armored brigade. Most of the infantrymen came from the elite *1ˢᵗ "Golani" Infantry Brigade* and the tanks were from the *188th "Barak" Armored Brigade*. The *188th Armored Brigade*, consisting of three slightly under strength battalions totaling about 90 tanks, manned positions along the Purple Line from north of Kuneitra to Rafid. Eleven field artillery batteries with a total of 44 pieces stood in the rear in support of these forward positions. These guns ranged in caliber from 105 millimeters to 155 millimeters, all self-propelled.[7]

The Syrian Offensive Plan

The overall Arab concept for the Ramadan War envisaged a two-front, coordinated offensive launched simultaneously in the Sinai, by the Egyptian led coalition, and on the Golan Heights, by the Syrian led coalition, under conditions of complete surprise. The aims of the Syrian Army were threefold. First, the Syrians sought to paralyze the Israeli command by saturating the Golan Heights with overwhelming combat power. Second, they wanted to destroy as much Israeli armor as possible by sustaining an attack along the entire length of the Golan Heights and not letting the Israelis rest or push in reinforcements. Third, the Syrians wanted to exploit their initial success by committing their two armored divisions to complete the breakthrough and recapture the Golan Heights.[8]

The Syrian plan was completely of their own design, though strongly influenced by the Soviet doctrine their officers had learned at Russian military academies. The Syrian offensive was planned to follow typical Soviet doctrine, with a few minor changes to fit the Syrian situation. First, the offensive was to begin with a short period of intense and violent firepower to shock the Israeli defenders. This was to be delivered by combining the effects of aircraft, artillery, tank, and mortar fire on key locations. The Syrians decided against a long period of fire in order for their attacking formations to take full advantage of the surprise and shock. Second the offensive would be launched on a broad front in order to force the widest possible dispersion of the Israeli defensive effort. Lastly, the Syrians would concentrate overwhelming combat power at two critical points to create two penetrations through the overextended Israeli defenses.[9] The Syrian leaders believed that a plan following this model would allow the Syrian Army to overrun the under strength Israeli defenses and capture the Golan Heights before the Israelis could mobilize and push reserves to the battlefront.

The Syrian attack plan called for a double breakthrough by the 7th Infantry Division (reinforced with an armored brigade) near Kuneitra in the north, and by the 5th Infantry Division (reinforced with an armored brigade) near Rafid in the south. A double envelopment of the bulk of the Israeli forces on the Golan Heights would occur once the breakthrough succeeded. The envelopment would be accomplished with the 7th Infantry Division continuing the attack west toward the northern Jordan River crossings, and the 5th Infantry Division moving on a parallel route toward the Arik Bridge just north of Lake Tiberias (the Arab name for the Sea of Galilee).[10]

In order to keep the Israelis pinned down all along the Purple Line, the 9th Infantry Division (reinforced with an armored brigade), in the center, would attack west between Kuneitra and Rafid. At the same time Brigadier General Safrawi's Moroccan Brigade would make a strong demonstration towards the foothills of Mt. Hermon to the north of the 7th Infantry Division. Both the 9th Infantry Division and the Moroccan Brigade were given limited objectives and were not to advance further without authority from General Headquarters in Damascus.[11]

The second echelon of the Syrian field army consisted of the 1st and 3rd Armored Divisions, which were to be used as the exploitation force once the breakthrough occurred. The 1st Armored Division would be the exploitation force if the 5th Infantry Division made a breakthrough, or if both the 5th and 7th Infantry Divisions were successful. The 1st Armored Division would drive between the 5th and 9th Infantry Divisions and attack towards Nafakh to the northern bridges over the Jordan River. However, if the 5th Infantry Division was unsuccessful and the 7th Infantry Division created the breakthrough then the 3rd Armored Division would become the exploitation force. The 3rd Armored Division would attack between the 7th and 9th Infantry Divisions toward Nafakh to capture the northern bridges over the Jordan River. In no case were both the 1st and 3rd Armored Divisions to be committed. One of them was to be held as a general reserve in the event of failure or unexpected developments.[12]

Syrian and Israeli Forces on the Eve of War

As the time for the attack neared, the Syrian Army began to move out of its defensive positions into attack positions and made the final preparations for the war that was about to begin. The Syrian Army habitually conducted field exercises during this time of the year so the Israelis were not overly concerning by the movement of forces opposite the Golan Heights. The Syrians left only 100 tanks in defensive positions around Damascus as a reserve. The Syrian Army massed some 70,000 soldiers organized in five divisions, two armored and three reinforced infantry, east of the Purple Line for its attack. In all, the Syrians fielded nearly 1,400 tanks (including 400 of the more modern T-62s), 950 artillery pieces ranging in caliber from 85 millimeters to 203 millimeters, at least 400 antiaircraft guns, and more than 100 batteries of SA-2, SA-3 and SA-6 surface-to-air missiles with between 400 and 500 launchers. In addition, the Syrian Air Force added over 300 combat aircraft to the fight. These included 110 MiG-21s, 120 MiG-17s, and 45 Su-7s.[13]

With the majority of the Israeli active duty forces deployed in the Sinai to counter the Egyptian Army massed along the Suez Canal, without mobilizing their reserves all the IDF could spare for the defense on the Golan Heights was the *188th Armored Brigade*. This brigade was equipped with modified Centurion tanks and had an under strength infantry brigade to man twelve of the seventeen fortified observation posts and strong points. As a backup, the Israelis maintained two armored divisions worth of equipment in emergency stores deployed below the Golan Heights. Just hours before hostilities began, as a measure of insurance in response to a Syrian military buildup in the Damascus basin, the *7th Armored Brigade* personnel were shifted from the Sinai to the Golan Heights and drew tanks and equipment from those emergency stores. The *7th Armored Brigade* was deployed behind the *188th Armored Brigade's* positions north of Kuneitra. In all the Israelis were able to put 12,000 combat and combat support soldiers, about 200 Centurion tanks (105 with the *7th Armored Brigade* and 90 with the *188th*

Armored Brigade), several dozen M3 half-tracks, several dozen M113s and 70 self-propelled artillery pieces of all calibers on the Golan Heights.[14]

Both the Syrian and Israeli forces faced a similar challenge--a short window of time to accomplish their missions. It was crucial that the Syrian attack reach the Jordan River bridges in time to block the Israeli reserves from coming to the rescue of the forces defending on the Golan Heights. Likewise, the Israeli defense had to hold out long enough for Israeli reserves to get to the battlefield to prevent the Syrians from effecting a breakthrough.

The Syrians rightly assessed the Israeli dispositions on the Golan Heights, estimating that less than 200 tanks were deployed against their 1,400. The plan was well designed and had an excellent chance of success.

The Final Preparations For War

To better understand the battle and the significant role that leadership played, it is necessary to review the strategic and operational setting and importance of the Golan Heights. During the 1967 Six-Day War, Israel quickly crushed the Syrian Army, pushing it off the Golan Heights. With the capture of the Golan, the Israeli Defense Force quickly realized its great strategic importance. Therefore, retention of the Golan became key and essential to the security of Israel.[15] The Golan Heights would now serve as a natural barrier to prevent invading Syrian forces from having easy access to the open desert of northern Israel. Because of the evident importance of the Golan Heights, the Israeli Defense Force was obviously very intent on retaining possession of this decisive piece of terrain.

The Syrians also saw the great importance of the Golan Heights and were as determined to reclaim the strategically important land as the Israelis were determined to keep it. To succeed the Syrians realized they would have to secretly mass their forces to avoid alerting the Israelis, who would then mobilize their reserves. They also grasped the necessity of seizing the Golan Heights in the first twenty-four to thirty-six hours of battle, before Israeli reserves could assemble and counterattack.[16] Therefore, the Syrians saw secrecy in planning and preparation as paramount to their success.

In September of 1973 the Syrians started to secretly assemble their forces just behind the Purple Line, which was the cease-fire line established at the end of the Six-Day War.[17] Despite extensive attempts at secrecy, on the 3rd of October 1973 Israeli intelligence had received numerous reports that Syria was moving additional troops into positions behind the Purple Line. Even with this intelligence the Israeli Defense Force hesitated to alert their army.

The reason for the hesitation by the Israeli Defense Force was twofold. First, neither the Israeli military nor the Israeli government believed Syria would attack after the decisive victory Israel achieved over the Arab armies in 1967. Second, 6 October was Yom Kippur, the holiest day of Judaism. To issue an alert would cause the recall of soldiers home on leave celebrating the holiday. The Israeli Defense Force did not declare "Alert Gimmel", the recall of all soldiers on leave and the mobilization of the reserves, until late on the fifth of October after observers saw Syrian forces massing east of the Purple Line with the clear intention to mount an attack against the Golan Heights. With the alert communicated so late in the day, many soldiers did not reach their units until the next morning, less than twelve hours before the Syrian attack.[18] Though the Syrians lost their advantage of complete surprise, they were able to keep the Israelis in the dark long enough that they failed to alert their reserves early enough to be in position to face the Syrian attack. This would give the Syrians at least twenty-four hours to seize the Golan Heights before the first Israeli reserves arrived.

The commander of the *Israeli Defense Force's Northern Command*, which has responsibility for the defense of the Golan Heights, was Major General Yitzhak Hofi. He was a paratrooper who had spent his entire adult life in the army. He was a veteran of innumerable combat episodes, beginning in the late 1940s. He had been a charter member of *Unit 101*, the ultra-elite commando force that countered Arab raids and served as a model and tactical test bed for the emerging IDF during the early and mid-1950s.[19]

Major General Hofi planned to contain the Syrian attack with the Israeli forces on hand for at least thirty-six hours. This would allow the reserves to mobilize, move to an assembly area and then launch a counterattack against the Syrian forces in the Golan Heights. Unlike his superiors at *Israeli Defense Force Headquarters*, Major General Hofi did not rule out a Syrian attack on the Golan Heights. In fact, it was Major General Hofi's mounting concern in late September that led to his request that the *77th Armored Battalion* from the *7th Armored Brigade* be reassigned to the Golan Heights to reinforce the *188th Armored Brigade* under his command.[20] The *77th Armored Battalion*, widely considered the finest tank battalion in the premier armored brigade in the Israeli Army, started arriving on the Golan Heights on the twenty-seventh of September. The remainder of the *7th Armored Brigade*, consisting of the *82nd Armored Battalion* and the *75th Mechanized Infantry Battalion*, did not arrive in their assembly areas on the Golan Heights until the early morning of the sixth of October, just hours before the Syrian attack was to begin.[21] The *75th Mechanized Infantry Battalion* was further augmented by elements of the *71st Armored Battalion* and the *Armor School Battalion* which was comprised of a few tanks operated by students and cadre hastily assembled from the *Israeli Defense Force Armor School*, both under the command of Lieutenant Colonel Menahem Ratess.[22]

The arrival of the *7th Armored Brigade* added depth to the over extended forces of the *188th Armored Brigade* deployed along the Purple Line. The *188th Armored Brigade* had four battalions deployed along this forty-mile main line of defense. Two light infantry battalions, the *17th Infantry* and the *50th Parachute*, manned seventeen reinforced bunkers along the cease-fire line. A squad of infantry with antitank weapons and an artillery forward observer team manned each bunker. Near each bunker were fighting positions for a platoon of tanks. The tanks of the *74th* and *53rd Armored Battalions* occupied these fighting positions. These positions were 2.5-meter-high elevated earth ramparts (specially designed for the Centurion main battle tank's nine degree gun depression) from which tanks in hull down positions could bring accurate fire to bear on any armor encroaching on the tank ditch below. Behind these four battalions were the three battalions of the *7th Armored Brigade* deployed in a tactical assembly area in reserve.[23] The defensive plan was a classic economy of force mission; contain the enemy with a small well-entrenched force, without giving up the strategic high ground, until a larger force could mobilize, assemble and counterattack.

Thirty-nine-year-old Colonel Yitzhak Ben-Shoham commanded the *188th Armored Brigade*, the Barak Brigade. He had been in command of the brigade for five months having taken command in May 1973. Born in Turkey, Colonel Ben-Shoham was a natural and charismatic leader who believed in and always set the example by leading from the front. He was truly admired by the soldiers in his command. He spent the last few days prior to the start of hostilities visiting his subordinate leaders and soldiers to ensure they knew the plan and knew what he expected of them in the upcoming battle.[24] The *188th Armored Brigade* consisted of the *53rd* and *74th Armor Battalions*. Lieutenant Colonel Oded Eres, who had only been in command for two weeks, commanded the *53rd*. Lieutenant Colonel Yair Nofshe, who was known as an excellent trainer of soldiers, commanded the *74th*. His battalion was battle ready as the hands of time ticked toward the upcoming war.[25]

    Colonel Avigdor Ben-Gal commanded the *7th Armored Brigade*. He was a seasoned combat veteran who was quiet and unassuming but who always led by example. Colonel Ben-Gal had proven himself as a commander of a tank company and later a tank battalion in previous wars.[26] Most importantly, he was highly regarded by his soldiers for his years of combat experience. From the first day Colonel Ben-Gal took command of the *7th Armored Brigade* he kept a chart on the war in his office titled *"DAYS TO GO TO WAR: REQUIRED PREPARATIONS."* He took every opportunity during training to personally address his soldiers, ensuring that they completely understood the purpose of their mission. He now made every effort to personally talk to his subordinate leaders and soldiers to impress upon them the importance of their success, stressing to them that failure could possibly lead to the collapse of Israel as a country.[27] This obviously provided a strong motivation for the soldiers of the *7th Armored Brigade* as they began to assemble on top of the Golan Heights in late September and early October 1973.

Colonel Ben-Gal's extensive combat experience told him that a static defense alone would probably not contain the enemy's attack. He prudently directed each tank battalion to keep one tank company in reserve behind their defensive positions once the brigade was committed. Additionally, Colonel Ben-Gal also maintained a tank company as the brigade reserve, under his direct command and control.[28] These reserve forces would give him great flexibility to counterattack any enemy forces that were able to penetrate the defensive line. The reserve could then reestablish the defensive positions to prevent further penetration. With multiple reserves, he could manage multiple incursions without his defense collapsing. Colonel Ben-Gal understood that above all he must hold the Golan Heights at all costs until reinforcements could be mobilized and moved to the front. Most importantly, Colonel Ben-Gal provided his soldiers with a clear purpose, strong motivation, and comprehensive directions on how to fight. His detailed guidance gave his unit confidence that they would accomplish their mission, imbuing them with the will to win.

Lieutenant Colonel Avigdor Kahalani commanded the *77th Armored Battalion*, known by its Hebrew numeric acronym of Oz, or "Courage." Lieutenant Colonel Kahalani was already a living legend within the IDF Armored Corps circles. He had returned from a life-threatening injury in the Six-Day War and was already one of the most decorated and commended soldiers ever to serve in the IDF.[29]

He also provided his soldiers with a clear purpose and direction. After moving into their assembly area on the morning of the sixth of October, Lieutenant Colonel Kahalani assembled his battalion's key leaders at his headquarters where he personally briefed them on the Syrian border situation and the battalion's mission, ensuring that everyone fully understood their part in the upcoming battle. Lieutenant Colonel Kahalani then escorted his company commanders back to their company assembly areas, where he visited with every platoon in his command. This allowed the soldiers in the battalion to see their leaders out forward with them. While trooping the platoon assembly areas he also took the time to quiz the junior leaders and soldiers on their role in the battle discussing every possible contingency that he could foresee and asking what actions they would take.[30] Because of Lieutenant Colonel Kahalani's leadership individual tank crews would continue to fight during the battle because they understood the importance of their tasks as part of the team. Furthermore, the soldiers fully comprehended what they had to do to accomplish their unit's mission. This would allow them to still take the appropriate actions even with the death of key leaders or the loss of radio communications.

Rounding out the *7th Armored Brigade* were the *82nd Armored Battalion* and the *75th Infantry Battalion*. The commander of the *82nd Armored Battalion* was Lieutenant Colonel Haim Barak. He was a veteran tank officer who had made a name for himself during the Six-Day War as a no-nonsense leader. He believed in the 3D philosophy of command (discipline, discipline and discipline) and demanded the 3A's from his men (accuracy, adherence to standards and absolute dedication to the mission). Lieutenant Colonel Yossi Eldar, commander of the *75th Infantry Battalion*, was a spit-and-polish disciplinarian who always led from the front. He had proven himself to be a gifted tactician and a courageous leader during the Six-Day War. Attached to the *75th Infantry Battalion* were remnants of the *71st Armored Battalion* and the tanks from the *Armor School Battalion* commanded by Lieutenant Colonel Meshulam Retes. He was a dedicated armor officer who had also proven his skills and courage during the Six-Day War.[31]

As the time for war drew near, the Israeli leaders on the Golan Heights had set the conditions for their eventual victory. The brigade and battalion commanders had instilled a clear sense of purpose in their soldiers, motivating them to fight for the survival of their country. Because of this, the soldiers of the *7th* and *188th Armored Brigades* completely understood what they had to do to accomplish their mission. In the absence of their leaders and facing overwhelming odds, they would continue to fight because they understood their role as part of the unit. Lastly, the soldiers would continue to fight because they understood the consequences if they failed.

The Syrians realized that a frontal attack in daylight would be costly. However, they were relying on overwhelming mass and firepower to break open the Israeli defense. To further their chances, the Syrians prepared elaborately for the attack, considering every possible contingency. Throughout the summer of 1973, the Syrians conducted extensive rehearsals of combined arms obstacle breaching with the support of Soviet advisors. In August, they even conducted a full force rehearsal on an exact replica of the Israeli defenses.[32] With the plan for the attack set in motion the Syrians were convinced that their attack would regain the Golan Heights.

This was the situation for both the Syrian and the Israeli forces on the Golan Heights at noon on 6 October 1973, just two hours before war was to erupt once again in the Middle East. The Golan Heights, scene of bitter fighting in the Six Day War, was about to witness a defensive action which would go down in history as one of the truly great defensive battles of all time, equal to the battle for the Somme in World War I or Mount Cassino in World War II.

---

[1] Avraham (Bren) Adan, *On The Banks of the Suez* (Presidio, California: Presidio Press, 1980), 67-68.

[2] Martin van Creveld, *The Sword and the Olive: A Critical History of the Israeli Defense Force* (New York: Public Affairs, 1998), 220-221.

[3] Chaim Herzog, *The Arab-Israeli Wars: War and Peace in the Middle East* (New York: Random House, 1982), 199.

[4] Trevor N. Dupuy, *Elusive Victory: The Arab-Israeli Wars, 1947-1974* (Fairfax, Virginia: Hero Books, 1984), 439.

[5] Ibid., 437.

[6] Kenneth M. Pollack, *Arabs At War: Military Effectiveness, 1948-1991* (Lincoln: University of Nebraska Press, 2002), 483-84.

[7] Jerry Asher and Eric Hammel, *Duel For The Golan: The 100-Hour Battle That Saved Israel* (New York: William Morrow and Company, Inc., 1987), 35-37.

[8] Ibid., 64.

[9] Pollack, *Arabs At War*, 482.

[10] Ibid., 483.

[11] Ibid., 484.

[12] Ibid., 484-85.

[13] Dupuy, *Elusive Victory*, 441.

[14] Ibid., 443.

[15] Samuel M. Katz, *Israeli Tank Battles: Yom Kippur to Lebanon* (London: Arms and Armor Press, 1988), 7.

[16] Kenneth M. Pollack, *Arabs At War: Military Effectiveness, 1948-1991* (Lincoln: University of Nebraska, 2002), 483.

[17] Jerry Asher and Eric Hammel, *Duel For The Golan: The 100-Hour Battle That Saved Israel* (New York: William Morrow and Company, Inc., 1987), 57.

[18]Ibid., 59.

[19]Ibid., 61.

[20]Ibid., 63.

[21]Katz, *Israeli Tank Battles*, 10.

[22]Avigdor Kahalani, *The Heights of Courage: A Tank Leader's War on the Golan* (London: Greenwood Press, 1984), 26.

[23]Samuel M. Katz, *Fire & Steel: Israel's 7th Armored Brigade* (New York: Pocket Books, 1996), 127.

[24]Asher and Hammel, *Duel for the Golan,* 66.

[25]Asher and Hammel, *Duel for the Golan,* 67-68.

[26]Katz, *Israeli Tank Battles*, 11.

[27]Katz, *Fire & Steel,* 134.

[28]Ibid., 135.

[29]Asher and Hammel, *Duel for the Golan,* 68.

[30]Kahalani, *The Heights of Courage*, 27.

[31]Katz, *Fire & Steel,* 128-130.

[32]Jac Weller, "Middle East Tank Killers," *Royal United Services Institute Journal* (December 1974): 12.

CHAPTER 2

THE BATTLE FOR THE GOLAN HEIGHTS

The Battle is Joined--Day 1

At approximately 1350 hours on 6 October, the Syrians initiated their attack with a fifty-minute artillery and air barrage of the Israeli command-and-control centers, military encampments, garrisons, vehicle parks, and key defensive positions. This tremendous barrage was a prelude to the Syrian two-pronged attack; the northern prong in the vicinity of the Kuneitra-Damascus road and the southern prong where Rafid bulges into Syria.[1] Syrian intelligence was excellent so they attacked in the right places; however, the execution of the attack was horrible. The Syrians estimated that the heavy volume of this bombardment, conducted by 655 artillery pieces and over 100 aircraft, would neutralize or destroy many of the defending Israeli forces.[2] Casualties amongst the defenders were light and little damage to equipment occurred. A few tank commanders sustained wounds while standing exposed in their commander's cupola.[3] While the barrage was heavy, it was mostly unobserved fire against dug-in tanks and artillery. Since artillery is generally ineffective against armored vehicles without a direct hit, the Israelis lost no tanks or artillery in the opening barrage.

The barrage did force the Israeli tank commanders to fight from inside their tanks with the hatches closed, restricting their view. It also destroyed radio antennas mounted on the outside of the Israeli tanks, preventing radio communication between tanks. Despite the wounding of several tank commanders and the loss of radio communications, there was no panic in the Israeli ranks.[4] However, the tank commanders knew the importance of staying in position and waiting for the Syrian tanks, and fought without further guidance because they clearly understood the plan. Every Israeli soldier knew they had to hold at all costs until the reserves could be mobilized and reinforcements arrived. Had the Israelis panicked and fled during the heavy bombardment, the battle may have turned into a rout. Instead, Israeli leadership set the conditions for the tank crews to brave the enemy fire and have the confidence to patiently hold their position until the enemy assault.

With the end of the bombardment of the Israeli defenses, the artillery shifted its fire to the vicinity of the planned breach sites in the obstacles along the tank ditch. No longer harassed by artillery, Israeli tank commanders emerged from their hatches to watch the Syrians begin their onslaught towards the tank ditch. From north to south the Syrian 7th, 9th and 5th Infantry Division, each reinforced with a brigade of armor, moved out of their hidden assembly areas just a few kilometers beyond the Purple Line to begin their attack. This huge mechanized formation of over 500 tanks and 700 armored personnel carriers raced towards the obstacle in Soviet march formation, breaking off into prebattle formation just one kilometer from the planned breach sites.[5] This vast armada of armored vehicles maneuvering towards them did not intimidate the Israeli defenders. Instead, they patiently waited for the Syrian tanks to get within range of their tank cannons.

The battle for the Golan Heights quickly turned into two distinct battles: the battle north of the Kuneitra Gap which was first fought by the *74th Armored Battalion* and then the *7th Armored Brigade*; and the battle south of the Kuneitra Gap fought initially by the *53rd Armored Battalion* and then the *188th Armored Brigade*. In order to tell the story of both battles nearly simultaneously the author will discuss the battles in the north and then in the south during distinct periods of time.

The Syrians took measures to obscure the breach sites, but not the movement of the forces to those sites. This was a serious mistake for which the Syrians would pay dearly because the planned breach lanes were around 1,500 meters from the Israeli tanks, which was the maximum effective range of the Centurion main battle tank's 105-millimeter main gun.[6] Therefore, the Syrians assumed that the Israelis would not engage them until they reached the obstacles. Realizing that they were greatly outnumbered, tank commanders in the *74th Armored Battalion* directed their gunners to begin firing when the Syrian tanks reached 3,000 meters. Despite the extended range, Israeli tanks started to kill the essential mine-clearing tanks and bridging vehicles. These long-range engagements were possible because of razor sharp skills the Israeli gunners had honed over years of experience and the confidence inspired by their leaders. Before the battle, Lieutenant Colonel Yair Nofshe, the commander of the *74th Armored Battalion*, continued a long Israeli tradition of promising the tank gunners a bottle of champagne for every enemy tank destroyed.[7] Instead of panic or despair, the Israeli tank crews remained calm and continued to fight with great skill stimulated by their leaders even as their own losses started to mount.

In the *74th Armored Battalion's* sector the burning hulks of Syrian vehicles quickly littered the area around the breach site. With the destruction of the key breaching vehicles and overall heavy casualties so soon in the battle, the Syrian attack might have failed. However, the Syrians dispatched dismounted engineers and infantry to dismantle the obstacles by hand. Though constantly harassed with Israeli artillery, the determined

Syrian infantry succeeded in breaching the Israeli obstacles by nightfall.[8] With the obstacles breached and the arrival of darkness, the Syrians began to gain the initiative since the Israeli Centurion tanks had no night vision capability like the Soviet-made T-55s and T-62s.

As darkness began to descend upon the Golan Heights on 6 October Lieutenant Colonel Nofshe quickly realized how serious the situation was. In the darkness, the Syrians would be able to expand their breach lanes and, using their night vision equipment, start advancing up the Golan Heights. He recognized that if he did not act quickly his defensive positions would soon be overwhelmed. At this point, he had two courses of action; withdraw his forces back to a subsequent defensive position and cede the high ground to the Syrians, or counterattack to close the breaches. Given the odds and the lack of night vision sights, it would seem the reasonable course of action would have been to withdraw. Nevertheless, Lieutenant Colonel Nofshe decided to counterattack. He immediately ordered his reserve company commander, Captain Avner Landau, to destroy enemy forces on the near side of the obstacle and to close the breaches.[9] In spite of the great difficulty of the assigned mission, Captain Landau's tank company quickly left its assembly area and maneuvered down the hill towards the enemy.

Leading a force of seven Centurion tanks, Captain Landau used the light provided from burning Syrian vehicles to guide his way down the slope. His company arrived at the breach site just as a Syrian tank company traversed the tank ditch. At a range of less than 200 meters, the Israelis destroyed fifteen Syrian tanks in only half an hour. With the enemy tanks near the breach destroyed, Captain Landau still needed to close the breach. However, Syrian infantry with antitank missiles promptly drove him away from the obstacle, damaging several of his tanks. Unable to close the breach and finding it too dangerous to stay where the infantry could range his tanks, Captain Landau withdrew his forces to the high ground.[10] Though not completely successful, Captain Landau had bravely led his company into battle at night against a numerically superior enemy equipped with night vision equipment. His personal fearlessness in the face of the enemy served to reassure his men, and they remained committed to holding back the Syrian attack.

There was more than one Syrian breach in the *74th Armored Battalion's* sector, so Lieutenant Colonel Nofshe ordered another one of his tank companies to counterattack. Captain Zvi Rock guided his company forward in two groups; seven tanks under his direct control and a tank platoon, with three tanks, under the command of Lieutenant David Eiland. Lieutenant Eiland slowly and carefully led his platoon forward in the dark over the broken, undulating ground, not knowing where the Syrians had breached the obstacle. Cresting a small rise just short of the tank ditch, Lieutenant Eiland found fifteen Syrian tanks and additional armored personnel carriers just 400 meters away. Lieutenant Eiland's platoon quickly destroyed all fifteen Syrian tanks and many of the armored personnel carriers without the loss of a single tank. The remainder of the enemy infantry and personnel carriers quickly dispersed after seeing the tank company destroyed.[11] Facing a numerically superior force, Lieutenant Eiland could have withdrawn and awaited the arrival of the rest of his company but instead of withdrawing he ordered his platoon to follow him in an attack.

Though greatly outnumbered, Lieutenant Eiland's platoon inflicted heavy casualties on the Syrian force. By keeping his platoon constantly moving and using the undulating terrain as concealment, the Syrian tanks were unable to engage the Israeli tank platoon. The Syrians responded by pushing forward infantry with antitank weapons to disrupt the Israeli attack and thus enable them to bring more armor through the breach. One of the Syrian infantry, a sniper, was able to kill Sergeant Nimrud Khochavi, one of Lieutenant Eiland's tank commanders. The crew of the tank reacted by driving off at full speed for the battalion's aid station, leaving Eiland with only two tanks. Sensing that he had lost the momentum of his attack, Lieutenant Eiland decided to pull back. Driving back uphill through the wadi system, Eiland inadvertently drove up on three Syrian tanks less than fifty meters away. Luckily, Lieutenant Eiland's gunner was more alert than the Syrian gunners, and quickly fired his 105-millimeter tank cannon three times, destroying all three Syrian tanks.[12] Lieutenant Eiland's platoon of three tanks was able to kill nineteen Syrian tanks that had crossed through the breach, but the breach still lay open.

Captain Rock arrived with the remainder of the company just as Lieutenant Eiland was withdrawing up the hill. Realizing that the area of the breach was occupied with Syrian infantry, Captain Rock was unwilling to risk the loss of his tanks. In such broken ground at night, dismounted infantry with antitank weapons had a clear advantage over tanks. Furthermore, Captain Rock had already lost one tank commander to sniper fire and could not afford to lose any more. For that reason, he moved his tanks further up the ridge to previously prepared positions around Bunker 109.[13] From this position his tank company could over watch the breach site and block any Syrian armor attempting to climb up the Golan Heights.

Once in position around Bunker 109, Captain Rock realized that his company was extremely low on fuel and ammunition. He decided to pull his tank out of the defensive line and personally drive to the battalion supply point. From there, he could lead the resupply vehicles forward to the company's position. Knowing that the Syrian infantry could have infiltrated deeper into the Israeli defense, Captain Rock took great risk in moving as a lone tank. To get to the resupply point Captain Rock had to zigzag across broken and undulating ground while under fire most of the way. It is a hallmark of Israeli leadership, though misguided, to seek personal danger before ordering others to take risks. After reaching the resupply point without incident, he found Sergeant Khochavi's tank and crew. The soldiers were lamenting the death of their leader and did not want to go back because they though it meant certain death. Captain Rock simply responded with "I'm going back." After loading his tank with supplies, Captain Rock watched as Sergeant Khochavi's tank pulled behind him and followed him back to the defense.[14] By showing courage and conviction in the face of danger he had swayed his men to continue to fight.

Thus, the first day of battle ended for the *74th Armored Battalion*. They had successfully contained the Syrian attack, though the breach lanes in the obstacle still lay open. The burning hulks of 59 Syrians tanks littered the near side of the obstacle, proving that few Syrians had successfully exploited the breaches. The battalion's losses were light, with one tank commander killed and several wounded. Artillery fire and glancing blows from Syrian tank cannon and antitank rockets damaged several tanks, while driving across the broken, rocky ground at night damaged a few more. The battalion was also critically low on fuel and ammunition.[15] While the battalion had won a great victory on this first day against overwhelming odds, the battle was not over yet.

The *74th Armored Battalion's* success was clearly due to the fearlessness of its leaders. Lieutenant Colonel Nofshe boldly ordered counterattacks against an enemy better equipped and greatly outnumbering him. The subsequent daring assaults led by two of his company commanders succeeded in destroying the majority of the enemy vehicles that had passed through the breaches, thus ensuring the temporary safety of the Israeli positions. In every instance, the Israeli tank commanders led from the front and set a personal example of courage in the face of the enemy. When soldiers expressed uncertainty or started to show signs of despair, their commanders rallied them by their personal presence and by leading by example. Israeli small unit leadership was unmistakably the decisive factor in this first day of battle.

While Lieutenant Colonel Nofshe's *74th Armored Battalion* was holding the defensive line in the 188th Brigade's northern sector, Lieutenant Colonel Oded Eres's *53rd Armored Battalion* was facing the Syrian onslaught in the brigade's southern sector. Lieutenant Colonel Eres concentrated the battalion's defenses around the Hushniya, Rafid and Tap Line roads. The terrain in the southern sector was not as rough as in the *74th Armor Battalion's* sector.[16] This caused two problems for the tanks of the *53rd Armor Battalion*. First, the Syrian armor was not nearly as canalized as in the north. This meant that Lieutenant Colonel Eres could not concentrate his forces at one or two vital choke points like Lieutenant Colonel Nofshe could in the north. Second, once the tanks of the *53rd* came out of their prepared positions to either reposition or counterattack, the terrain did not provide as many natural hull-down fighting positions for protection against Syrian tank and missile fire.

Lieutenant Colonel Eres chose to dissect his sector placing Captain Uri Akavia's company north of the Tap Line road to cover Bunkers 110, 111 and 113 with a platoon each. These bunkers blocked access to the Hushniya road and the Arik Bridge over the Jordan River. He placed Captain Avi Roni's company in the south to cover Bunkers 114, 115 and 116 with a platoon each. These bunkers blocked access to the Rafid and Tap Line roads. Captain Uzi Ureali's company was designated the battalion reserve, under the control of the battalion deputy commander, Major Shmuel Askarov.[17] Keeping a reserve force this large, a third of his fighting force, was risky but it provided Lieutenant Colonel Eres the flexibility to either bolster any area of the defense seriously threatened or to counterattack any penetrations by the Syrians.

The tank platoon in support of Bunker 111 was the first to report contact. Captain Akavia moved his tank into a position to support the platoon by controlling the target acquisition and fire distribution. Long-range fire accounted for the first four tanks of the Syrian 9th Infantry Division's reinforced 53rd Infantry Brigade. Captain Akavia's first report to Lieutenant Colonel Eres estimated that his four Centurions were facing between forty and sixty tanks and armored personnel carriers, and he asked for help.[18]

Lieutenant Colonel Eres ordered Major Askarov to lead one of the platoons held in reserve to assist in the battle that raged around Bunker 111. Major Askarov's contingent of four tanks arrived just in time to take part in the destruction of six more Syrian tanks. This brought the total of Syrian tanks destroyed to ten without the loss of a single Israeli soldier or tank.[19]

The Syrians now threw twenty-five tanks against the eight Israeli tanks defending around Bunker 111. Both Major Askarov and Captain Akavia continued to control the fire distributions of their force. The Israeli tank crews fired only on direct orders continuing to score hits at long range. As the Syrian tanks continued to close on the bunker complex the Israeli gunners naturally picked up the pace and in time a free-for-all developed. As the battle raged around Bunker 111 Israeli losses started to mount. During these last engagements five Israeli tanks, including the company commander's and both platoon leader's tanks, were destroyed by volley fire from the Syrian T-55s 100-millimeter guns.[20]

As darkness fell the Syrians pulled back leaving thirty-five armored vehicles burning or abandoned between Tel Kudna and Bunker 111, though they had inflicted grievous casualties upon the Israelis.[21] As Major Askarov reorganized his defenses he realized that he was down to just three Centurion tanks and only sixty-nine 105-millimeter tank rounds. At this point he directed his tank commanders to only fire tank rounds at other tanks; armored personnel carriers were to be engaged only with heavy machine guns. Also, in a desperate hope of bluffing the Syrians into believing that reinforcements were arriving he ordered his driver to run his tank back and forth to raise dust, taking a page out of Field Marshal Rommel's North African playbook.[22]

Though Major Askarov had won the first round, he remained apprehensive about continuing the action into the night because he knew his Centurion tanks did not have the advantage of night vision sights like the T-55s. If the Syrians renewed their assault it would be a long night around Bunker 111 and would require reinforcements for the Israeli defense to hold.

The other six remaining tanks of Captain Avakia's company were strung out along the Tap Line Road under the command of Lieutenant Boaz Tamir. As a column of

Syrian tanks thrust toward Lieutenant Tamir's sector the Israeli gunners quickly destroyed the two leading tanks, but the Syrian tanks just kept grinding forward in what seemed to be inexhaustible numbers. The Israelis continued to score direct hits as the range between the two forces closed to less than three hundred meters. However, this close quarter fighting cost Lieutenant Tamir four of his six Centurion tanks.[23] Lieutenant Tamir realized that he would not be able to stem the Syrian attack without reinforcements.

Up to this point in the battle Lieutenant Colonel Eres had managed to maintain the bulk of Captain Uzi Ureali's company in reserve. He did this despite repeated calls for assistance from several sectors and the news of mounting losses.

In the very southern sector of the *188th Armored Brigade* Captain Avi Roni was with his company's forward tank platoon on the Rafid Road. Like Captain Akavia and Major Askarov in the north, Captain Roni was controlling the fire distribution of his gunners.[24] Captain Roni quickly realized the magnitude of the Syrian assault. He pointedly told Lieutenant Colonel Eres that this was not a raid but an assault, an all out war. Shortly after giving this assessment he was killed by Syrian tank fire while trying to reposition his tank to a better position from which to control the raging battle.[25]

It now fell on Lieutenant Netaniel Aharon, deputy commander of Captain Roni's company, to stem the tide of the Syrian armored assault on Bunker 116 with four Centurion tanks and his command armored personnel carrier. Like most of his fellow commanders he controlled and distributed fire from his Centurions engaging the advancing T-55s with long-range fire from their rampart positions. Unlike similar stands in the north, Lieutenant Aharon's tiny force succeeded in keeping elements of the

Syrian's 5th Infantry Division's 61st Infantry Brigade in check at distances of two to three kilometers. Before the sunlight faded the platoon had managed to destroy eight Syrian T-55s at the cost of one Centurion.[26]

While perhaps not quite as intense as the fighting in Lieutenant Colonel Nofshe's northern sector, Lieutenant Colonel Eres's *53rd Armored Battalion* had fought a model defensive stand. Nearly sixty Syrian tanks and numerous armored personnel carriers had been destroyed in the southern sector of the Golan Heights before nightfall. Unlike the *74th Battalion*, however, the *53rd Battalion* had taken a beating. A dozen of the battalion's thirty Centurion tanks had been destroyed and two of the three company commanders were dead.[27] Reinforcements were urgently required if the Israelis were going to hold.

By 1630 on the sixth of October Brigadier General Raful Eitan, commander of the *36th Armored Infantry Division*, realized that the remaining tanks of the *188th Armored Brigade* were not going to be able to hold the Syrian onslaught and were in danger of being overwhelmed. He immediately issued orders committing the 105 Centurions of Colonel Ben-Gal's crack *7th Armored Brigade* to the fight.[28]

Reorganization of the Forces on the Golan Heights

Since control of the northern sector was crucial to the defense of the Golan Heights, Brigadier General Eitan ordered the *7th Armored Brigade* to assume responsibility for the vital area from Bunker 107 northward. This placed the key Kuneitra Gap within Colonel Ben-Gal's domain. At the same time, the depleted *188th Armored Brigade's* responsibility was narrowed to the southern sector already being defended by Lieutenant Colonel Eres's *53rd Armored Battalion*.[29]

Brigadier General Eitan realized he did not have time for reshuffling positions; he merely swapped units between the two brigades. Lieutenant Colonel Nofshe's *74th Armored Battalion* was operationally transferred from the *188th Armored Brigade* to the *7th Armored Brigade* control. In return, the *188th Armored Brigade* gained operational control of Lieutenant Colonel Barak's *82nd Armored Battalion* (minus one company that Colonel Ben-Gal retained as the brigade reserve) and two companies of Lieutenant Colonel Eldar's *75th Infantry Battalion* from the *7th Armored Brigade*.[30] Breaking up habitual relationships between units is never the preferred method because of the problems it causes in command and control, and the stress it places on commanders and soldiers at all levels. However, the tactical situation on the Golan Heights gave Brigadier General Eitan no choice. The Israeli army's ability to form ad hoc units on the fly and over come these inherent difficulties was a strength demonstrated during previous wars and would prove to be invaluable in this war also.

Colonel Ben-Gal's *7th Armored Brigade* had had a relatively quiet afternoon as it sat behind the main defensive line of the *188th Armored Brigade* waiting to be committed to battle. Once the order to move was given the units of the *7th Armored Brigade* were moving into their battle positions as quickly as possible. By 1700 hours Lieutenant Colonel Kahalani's *77th Armored Battalion* was occupying the tank ramparts between the Kuneitra Gap and the Hermonit awaiting the onslaught of Syrian armor they fully expected after darkness fell.[31]

At the same time the two companies of the *82nd Armored Battalion*, minus the battalion commander, linked up with Lieutenant Colonel Eres so he simply assumed command of the fresh tank companies. His plan was to use these two fresh companies and the remainder of his reserves to reinforce his depleted defenses.[32] Lieutenant Colonel Eres directed Major Dan Pesach, the battalion's deputy commander to take Captain Dan Levine's company of ten Centurions south to reinforce Lieutenant Aharon's tiny force at Bunker 116. He ordered his reserve of seven Centurions under Captain Ureali to bolster Lieutenant Tamir's desperate position along the Tap Line Road covering Bunker 114 in the center of the battalion's sector. Then he personally led Captain Eli Geva's company to conduct a sweep along the Rafid Road and reinforce the dwindling forces of Major Askarov around Bunker 111 in the north.[33]

Both Captains Ureali and Geva began their counterattack immediately. Captain Ureali's seven tanks arrived at Bunker 114 just as Lieutenant Tamir was down to his last two tanks. The nine Israeli tanks quickly destroyed 15 T-55s to temporarily stabilize the situation in the center of the battalion's sector. Captain Geva's company rapidly made its way up the Rafid Road reaching the Purple Line within an hour of reporting to Lieutenant Colonel Eres. Along the way Captain Geva's company destroyed twenty Syrian tanks and armored personnel carriers for the cost of one Centurion. He linked up with Major Askarov integrating his nine tanks into the defense around Bunker 111.[34] Both counterattacks were very successful making matters in the center and north look better than they had in hours. However, the situation in the south was about to go from bad to worse.

Major Pesach's force moved quickly southward toward Bunker 116 along the El Al Road. Major Pesach quickly deployed Captain Levine's company in blocking positions around the village of Ramat Magshamim to deny any advancing Syrians access to the strategic El Al Ridge. Lieutenant Colonel Eres thought this position was too far removed from the battlefield and ordered Captain Levine to Tel Juhadar in order to block any penetration along the Tap Line Road.[35] Captain Levine began his movement immediately and in the interest of speed he failed to employ scouts or flank protection. The result was one of the worst disasters ever inflicted upon Israel's armored corps.

A Syrian force of tanks and antitank weapons from the 5th Infantry Division's 132nd Mechanized Brigade had penetrated the front and had set up an ambush in well-concealed positions just south of Tel Juhadar. Captain Levine's was leading the company and his tank was the first to be destroyed. The company never regained control of the situation and all ten Centurions were destroyed in less than two minutes.[36]

As darkness fell over the Golan Heights on the sixth of October Brigadier General Eitan had the following picture: In the north the *7th Armored Brigade's* tanks were in prepared positions. The *77th Armored Battalion* had been relatively untouched and the *53rd Armor Battalion* was still in heavy contact but the situation was stable for the moment. The situation in the *188th Armored Brigade's* sector however was very disconcerting. The brigade was under attack by hundreds of Syrian tanks and their own tank strength was dwindling quickly. It was evident that the Syrians had managed three major penetrations in the south. In the south around Bunker 116 over one hundred tanks had broken through the Israeli defenses, while on the Rafid road another 100 tanks had penetrated as far as the Tap Line road. In the area of bunkers 114 and 115 an undetermined force of tanks and infantry was breaking in.[37] As bad as the situation was, it would have been much worse had it not been for the heroic actions, and the bold and timely decisions made by the small-unit leaders throughout the day.

Stubborn Defense in the North and Breakthrough in the South

As darkness fell the Syrians renewed their attacks in an attempt to break through in the *77th Armored Battalion's* sector. In the north the Syrian 68th and 58th reinforced Infantry Brigades of the 7th Infantry Division attempted to penetrate between the Booster and Hermonit while in the south 78th Armored Brigade of the 9th Infantry Division attempted to push through the Kuneitra Gap. Due to the fact that the Israeli Centurion tanks were not equipped with efficient night vision sights, Lieutenant Colonel Kahalani ordered his forces not to fire until the Syrian tanks were within 800 meters.[38]

From their ramparts the Israeli gunners could not see the tank ditch at night once the supply of artillery illumination rounds were expended. The Syrian infantry and engineers took advantage of this, breaching the obstacle in several places. The Syrian tanks attacked in waves as soon as they crossed through the breaches in the tank ditch. As the Syrian tanks came within short range, the Israeli tank commanders could clearly make out the T-55 infrared lights by looking through their infrared binoculars. On order the Israeli gunners opened fire with stunning effect destroying a dozen Syrian tanks within seconds. The Syrians quickly recovered, rallied, and continued their push forward opening fire with their 10-millimeter cannons at less than a 300-meter range with deadly effect. As the Syrians continued to close on the Israeli positions, tanks were engaging each other at ranges of less than 50-meters. The night was lit up as Israeli and Syrian tanks and many armored personnel carriers caught fire and blew up.[39]

While the fighting on top the Golan Heights continued, a force of at least a tank battalion had crossed through the breach and defended the foothold. Lieutenant Colonel Kahalani quickly recognized that because his gunners could not engage at long range at night he could not close the gap in the breach from his positions high on the Golan Heights. He realized he had to do something or his defenses would be overrun by the sheer mass of the advancing Syrian armor.

Once the situation on top of the Golan Heights was secure, Lieutenant Colonel Kahalani left a tank company in the battalion's defensive position and personally led the rest of his battalion on a counterattack to push the Syrians back across the obstacle.[40] This part of the Golan Heights was even more rocky and rugged than the *74th Armored Battalion's* sector, and visibility was limited to a few hundred meters. To assist in the counterattack, Lieutenant Colonel Kahalani repeatedly called for illumination from the artillery batteries, but they soon ran out of illumination rounds.[41] The battalion continued the counterattack through the darkness against an enemy equipped with night vision equipment in order to destroy the Syrian tanks west of the Purple Line.

First Sergeant Amir Bashari, one of the tank commanders, was the first to engage the enemy, spotting them from a ridge above the breach site. His gunner fired continuously at the numerous targets, destroying ten Syrian tanks in a matter of minutes. However, First Sergeant Bashari neglected to move after shooting and a Syrian tank round hit his turret, killing him instantly. Meanwhile, Lieutenant Colonel Kahalani continued to move his tanks forward, eventually closing to within 300 meters of the Syrian position.[42] The Israeli tank commanders knew that the Soviet T-55s were equipped with infrared searchlights, which they could use to spot enemy tanks at night. Their only hope was to close in to such a short range that they could acquire the Syrian tanks with their white light Xenon searchlights or the naked eye.

Once they were in position, Lieutenant Colonel Kahalani's unit began a dangerous cat and mouse game with the Syrians. One Israeli tank would use its spotlight to illuminate the Syrian position while another tank would engage any available targets. Both tanks would have to immediately change position after using this tactic, usually under a hail of Syrian fire. With all this shifting of forces, Lieutenant Colonel Kahalani and his wingman found themselves parked beside a tank with its taillights on. Unsure if it was friendly or enemy, he called all of his company commanders to make sure their lights were out. When all of the company commanders confirmed that their lights were out, Lieutenant Colonel Kahalani noticed that the unidentified tank still had its lights on. Assuming it was enemy but unwilling to shoot unless he could confirm it, he trained his gun on the tank while his wingman illuminated it. The searchlight confirmed it was a T-55, and Lieutenant Colonel Kahalani's gunner instantly destroyed it. The burning hulk revealed another T-55 less than 100 meters away, and his wingman immediately destroyed it.[43] Instead of staying back behind the fighting, Lieutenant Colonel Kahalani led from the front, setting an example of valor in combat for his soldiers to emulate.

By 0300, the Syrians halted their attempts to enlarge the foothold. In the area between the Booster and Hermonit over forty knocked out Syrian tanks were counted while around the Kuneitra Gap more than thirty additional armored vehicles lay strewn where they had attempted to break through.[44] Lieutenant Colonel Kahalani grasped the danger of continuing to fight in the dark, and pulled his battalion back to the ramparts. Moving into a position that over watched the breach site, he was determined to crush the Syrians when they attacked again at first light.

In the mean time, he understood the necessity of letting some of the soldiers sleep and taking time to repair tanks damaged while crossing the rough terrain. Wounded soldiers, mostly tank commanders, also needed medical treatment. One of the company commanders, Captain Menahem Albert, had received a nasty gash on his forehead from artillery shrapnel earlier in the day. Allowing his gunner to bandage his head, he refused to relinquish his command or be evacuated to the battalion aid station despite profuse bleeding.[45]

The *77th Armored Battalion* was successful in its first day of battle because of the great courage of its leaders. The soldiers continued to fight because they followed the example of their leaders, and when leaders were killed subordinate leaders stepped up to take control. The *77th* was victorious so far, but Lieutenant Colonel Kahalani knew the Syrians were still determined to drive him off the Golan Heights and would be back in the morning. The war was not going as well in the south with the *188th Armored Brigade*.

As darkness fell the situation in the *188th Armored Brigade's* sector was becoming desperate with two brigades of the 9th Infantry Division attacking in the north and the reinforced 5th Infantry Division attacking in the south. To hold back this onslaught the *188th Armored Brigade* could muster only eighteen tanks that were running dangerously low on ammunition: nine tanks north of Bunker 111 under Major Pesach (including Colonel Ben-Sholam's tank), six tanks around Bunker 114 overlooking the Tap Line Road under the command of Lieutenant Colonel Eres and at Bunker 111 in the south Lieutenant Gur had three Centurions.[46]

Colonel Ben-Shoham decided to move his advanced headquarters from Nafekh to Juhader where he could better control the battle. As his headquarters moved southwards the forces they met en route were already running out of ammunition. As he grasped the seriousness of the situation, he called for his personal tank to move from Hushniyah and join him.[47]

As Colonel Ben-Shoham left Nafekh, Lieutenant Zvi "Zwicka" Greengold pulled in. He had been assigned to a Company Commanders' Course and in preparation for the course had been sent on two weeks leave. Upon hearing the news of the war, he had donned his uniform and hitchhiked to Nafekh to rejoin his unit. Arriving at the same time were four tanks, three of which had been damaged and repaired, and he was given command over these tanks. Colonel Ben-Shoham ordered Lieutenant Zwicka to join him at Juhader.[48]

En route to link up with his brigade commander Lieutenant Zwicka ran into the same force that had destroyed Captain Levine's company earlier in the day. The Israeli gunners quickly destroyed six T-55s but at the cost of two Centurions. Lieutenant Zwicka broke contact choosing to site his tanks in good hull-down positions and wait for the enemy to continue its advance up the road. When Colonel Shoham received the report that Lieutenant Zwicka was in contact west of Tap Line Road he realized he was surrounded. Cut off from his troops and isolated, Colonel Shoham spoke to all the forces in a quiet and encouraging manner, urging them to hold on and promising them that help would be arriving soon.[49] Even though the situation was clear to the remnants of the brigade they would continue to fight to the last round, tank and man. The soldiers did so because their leaders had ensured that they understood their mission; they had to buy time for the reserves to arrive.

Shortly after settling into their positions Lieutenant Zwicka observed a column of T-55s from the 51st Independent Armored Brigade's 452nd Armored Battalion approaching. The Israeli gunners fired the first shots at a very close range destroying the two lead Syrian tanks. While repositioning, he and his wingman crested a hill and were immediately engaged by three Syrian tanks at point blank range. With three rapid shots three T-55s went up in flames, but the Syrians tanks had killed Lieutenant Zwicka's wingman also. Lieutenant Zwicka was now on his own with an enemy tank battalion roaming the area. He took up another good hull-down position and waited for the enemy to come to him. He did not have long to wait. Half an hour later he observed a column of thirty Syrian tanks accompanied by trucks driving along in perfect formation as if on parade. He allowed the lead tank to close to within 30 meters before he opened fire destroying the lead tank. He then proceeded to play cat and mouse with the Syrian force, popping up from behind a hill, firing, destroying a tank, and then repositioning. He continued to fight this way, eluding the Syrian tanks who thought they had run into a sizable Israeli force, causing the Syrian convoy to withdraw. The Syrians left ten burning T-55s behind.[50]

Just at this moment the first seven tanks of the *17th Reserve "Ran's" Brigade* arrived at Nafekh under the command of Lieutenant Colonel Uzi. These were the first reserve tanks to arrive on the Golan Heights. Colonel Ben-Shoham ordered him to link up with Lieutenant Zwicka and endeavor to push the Syrians back along Tap Line Road. The force was divided up with Lieutenant Colonel Uzi taking five tanks southwards along Tap Line Road and Lieutenant Zwicka with his three tanks parallel to them. When fire opened up on his force from two directions Lieutenant Colonel Uzi realized that his force had driven into a trap. For almost three hours his small force waged a hopeless battle against an enemy that greatly outnumbered them. Although his unit made a major contribution in buying time by holding up the Syrian advance during those critical hours, Lieutenant Colonel Uzi's unit was wiped out.[51]

Meanwhile, Lieutenant Zwicka pulled his three Centurions back into positions along the road hoping to pull off another ambush like he had earlier. Before he knew what was happening his tank was hit, throwing him from the tank with his clothes on fire. After he put the flames out he ran to a nearby tank. Just as he took command of this tank two Syrian tanks appeared in front of him. He fired two rounds at point blank range in quick succession destroying both T-55s.[52]

As the sun was coming up on the morning of the seventh of October, the situation in the 188th Armored Brigades sector was critical. The brigade could muster only fifteen Centurion tanks: Lieutenant Zwicka's two just southeast of Nafekh, twelve commanded by Lieutenant Colonel Eres around Juhader and the brigade commander's just north of Ramat Magshimim. The Syrian 5th Infantry Division had broken through the Israeli defenses in two locations during the night. In the center of the *188th Armored Brigade's* sector the 46th Armored Brigade had punched a hole in the defenses in the Rafid area that was quickly exploited by the 132nd reinforced Infantry Brigade. This is the force that Lieutenant Zwicka had been fighting all night and remnants of this brigade were now astride the Tap Line Road southeast of Nafekh. In the south the 47th Armored Brigade had overrun Bunker 116 and continued west practically unhindered. The battalions of this brigade stopped for the night just to the east of Yehudia, Gamla Rise and El Al. As the sun came up, the soldiers of this brigade looked down in amazement at the breath-taking view of the Sea of Galilee.[53] They realized that victory was almost within their grasp.

The Seventh of October--A Near Run Thing

In the north, as the sun began to rise the Syrian 7th Infantry Division clung doggedly to the established breach lanes. While the Syrian commanders had hoped for a larger foothold on the Israeli side of the obstacle, they decided to continue the attack as planned. With the arrival of first light just after 0400 hours, Syrian artillery initiated a heavy bombardment along the *7th Armored Brigade's* position. Under the cover of the artillery fire, the Syrian's 7th Infantry Division's uncommitted 78th Tank Brigade rushed the breaches at high speed and started the ascent to the top of the Golan.[54] The Israeli's gunners were hard pressed to deal with the ferocity and mass of the Syrian tank charge.

Though the Israelis quickly inflicted heavy losses on the attacking enemy, the Syrians simply kept coming without hesitation. A wild melee of tank on tank fighting ensued as the Syrians rapidly closed on the Israeli defensive positions. Despite the Syrian numbers, the Israeli leaders were able to bring the skill and daring of Israeli tank crews to bear and the tide started to turn. By 1300 hours, the 78th Tank Brigade ceased to exist as a unit, with over 90 burning tanks scattering the ridgeline. However, the *7th Armored Brigade* also suffered serious losses, with only 35 tanks remaining out of the brigade's original 105.[55] Once again, the bravery of Israeli tank commanders had averted disaster and defeated a significantly numerically superior enemy.

The Syrians were more successful on this attack for several reasons besides sheer mass. During the night, Syrian bulldozers continued to reduce the Israeli tank ditch, allowing more vehicles to cross simultaneously. A bridging tank had created another crossing where the tank ditch still stood. Additionally, Syrian artillery continued to bombard the Israeli positions throughout the attack and did not shift away to obscure the breach. The constant artillery suppression forced the Israeli tank commanders to fight inside their turrets, which limited their observation. The Syrians also coordinated several air attacks against the Israeli positions.[56] While the artillery and air attacks did not destroy a single Israeli tank, it forced the tank commanders to button up which limited their ability to observe and engage the mass of advancing Syrian tanks.

As before, Israeli leadership proved decisive in destroying the Syrian attack. As Lieutenant Colonel Kahalani looked across a sea of burning vehicles on the battlefield, he wondered what made his men so brave.[57] Much of their bravery and resolve came directly from him. Throughout the battle, Lieutenant Colonel Kahalani remained calm and cool on the radio, never sounding fearful, just as the *188th Armored Brigade* commander had done. He realized that in modern day battle where forces are spread over a large area the only way a commander can influence his soldiers is via the radio. He knew he had to keep talking quietly and calmly, as they were used to hearing him. He carefully directed his forces to counter the Syrian gains, sometimes even when all he had was an individual tank to close a gap in the line. Never did he show fear or despair, always remaining calm on the radio while encouraging his soldiers to hold the line. Throughout the battle, Kahalani positioned his tank in the center of the line, leading by example by personally destroying numerous enemy tanks. Lieutenant Colonel Kahalani's men were brave because he was brave.

The *77th Armored Battalion's* subordinate commanders also set an example of fearlessness for their soldiers. In the H Company sector, a T-55 found a well-concealed firing position about 800 meters from the Israeli defense. From this position in the low ground, the Syrian tank continually sniped at the Israeli tanks as they changed position. However, the Israeli's could not depress their gun tubes low enough to engage the Syrian tank without pulling forward out of the protection of their revetments. The company commander, Captain Emmy, decided he could not let the Syrian tank persist at harassing his defense. Driving his tank out into the open to a position where he could fire, he stayed exposed for several minutes until his gunner destroyed the Syrian tank.[58] All of the other officers in Captain Emmy's company were already dead, yet he continued to fight with great daring. His men simply followed his example.

With the destruction of his 78th Armored Brigade, Syrian Brigadier General Omar Abrash, the 7th Infantry Division commander, decided to wait for the hours of darkness to attempt another breakthrough, not realizing that the Israeli *7th Armored Brigade* was down to just thirty-five Centurion tanks.[59] Lieutenant Colonel Kahalani took advantage of the pause to ensure his tanks were resupplied and repositioned for the fight that was sure to come when darkness fell once again. He also realized that with the situation in the south the first reinforcements would go to reinforce the *188th Armored Brigade* and not his battalion.

While the *7th Armored Brigade* was able to repulse the continuing efforts of the Syrian 7th and 9th Infantry Divisions in the north, the story in the *188th Armored*

Brigade's sector in the south continued to be much different. The remnants of the 188th Armored Brigade were fighting a number of scattered, isolated, and uncoordinated defensive actions against elements of the 9th and the 5th Infantry Divisions. The Israelis were being slowly pushed back westward toward the escarpment and northwestward into the central Golan Heights past Hushniyah and toward Nafekh.[60] Aware of the desperate situation in the *188th Armor Brigade's* sector, Major General Hofi ordered mobilizing reserve units to move to the front as soon as they were ready, without waiting to concentrate in battalion or brigade formations.[61]

The Syrian commander and Chief of the General Staff, Major General Yousef Chakour, realized that 5th Infantry Division had penetrated the Israeli defense in the south between Rafid and Kudneh. He committed the 1st Armored Division, reinforced with the 141st Armored Brigade from General Headquarters Forces, to exploit this gap. 1st Armored Division was ordered to drive to the Jordan and Huleh Valleys through Hushniyah, Nafekh and the Bnot Ya'akov Bridge.[62] The only good news for the *188th Armored Brigade* was that reinforcements were beginning to arrive, even if they were only arriving piecemeal.

At 0520 hours Lieutenant Colonel Ran Sarig, Commander of the *Northern Command Tank Battalion*, led the last tanks of his battalion across the Arik Bridge. He planned to lead his Centurions in a counterattack against the Syrians last reported to be at the crossroads of the Hushniya and Tap Line Roads. However, as Lieutenant Colonel Sarig reached the escarpment, just five kilometers east of the Arik Bridge, he and his battalion ran into fifteen T-55s from the 9th Infantry Division's 51st Independent Tank Brigade. The two forces did not see each other until they very nearly collided. Gunners from both sides opened fire at point blank range as the two forces deployed into the fields on either side of the road. The Israeli gunners made quick work of the fifteen T-55s, destroying all of them just west of the Kuzabia crossroads, at the cost of one of their own Centurions.[63]

As this fight was going on in the south, Colonel Ben-Shoham and his small command group were making their way back to Nafekh to reestablish the brigade headquarters there. While en route he continued to receive bad news from around his sector. Just after 0600 hours Lieutenant Colonel Eres reported that the remnants of his *53rd Armored Battalion* were incapable of holding the Rafid Gap any longer and asked for permission to concentrate his waning tank force around Tel Faris.[64] At the same time Lieutenant Colonel Yair Laron's *50th Parachute Battalion* reported that it could no longer hold the El Al Ridge.[65]

About the same time Colonel Ben-Shoham and his command group arrived in Nafekh, Lieutenant Tamir was commanding the only Centurion remaining on the Tap Line Road near the Purple Line. He reported a formation of about sixty Syrian tanks moving in his direction and requested reinforcements from Lieutenant Colonel Eres. His battalion commander, also involved in heavy contact, could only afford to send the Lieutenant one tank and a half-track. Lieutenant Tamir's two tanks waited for the Syrian tanks to close and started firing. They destroyed several T-55s but then several volleys hit both Centurions from the onrushing enemy tanks. One tank was severely damaged but managed to escape back in the direction of Nafekh, while Lieutenant Tamir's tank was destroyed by five direct hits in quick succession.[66] The Syrians had bludgeoned an opening on the Tap Line Road and the route to Nafekh was basically wide open.

Upon hearing this news Colonel Ben-Shoham decided that with Lieutenant Zwicka's small force fighting along the Tap Line Road and Lieutenant Colonel Eres's force isolated at Tel Faris he needed to go out and fight on the Tap Line Road. Encouraging his forces to hold at all costs, the brigade commander, with his operations officer on board, headed out along Tap Line Road to link up with Lieutenant Zwicka's force. Immediately after Colonel Ben-Shoham departed Nafekh the first elements of Colonel Uri Orr's *679th Armored Brigade*, which had been rushed piecemeal to the Golan Heights, began to arrive. Major Dov, the *188th Armored Brigade's* intelligence officer, stood on the road by a half-track and began organizing the tanks that arrived into platoons of three. Major Dov managed to organize two companies worth of Centurions and reestablish the *188th Armored Brigades'* headquarters at Nafekh.[67]

Shortly after noon Colonel Ben-Shoham made contact with T-62s that were the elements of the 1st Armored Division's 91st Armored Brigade attacking along the Tap Line Road toward Nafekh. He reported destroying eight Syrian tanks as his second in command, Lieutenant Colonel David Yisraeli pulled up with three tanks he had collected from the brigade's repair shop. The brigade commander and his tiny command group of four tanks fought for several hours accounting for another sixteen destroyed tanks. The command group tanks began to run low on ammunition and were eventually overwhelmed by the sheer mass of Syrian armor. Colonel Ben-Shoham, his second-in-command, and his operations officer were killed on the outskirts of Nafekh buying precious time for reinforcements to arrive.[68] The time bought by Colonel Ben-Shoham and his beleaguered forces had allowed larger elements of the *240th Armored Division*, under the command of Major General Dan Laner, to arrive at the Arik and the Bnot

Ya'akov Bridges and the lead elements of the *146th Armored Division* to arrive in the south near El Al.[69]

However, the Syrian 1st Armored Division continued its march toward Nafekh. As the lead elements approached the camp two trackless Centurions, which were in the camp's repair shop, took up the fight. These two immobile tanks destroyed several Syrian T-62 tanks as they broke through the wire in a last ditch effort. This gained a momentary reprieve as the Syrian tanks hesitated. Just as all seemed lost a small tank column arrived at the camp and joined the fight. It was the vanguard of the *679th Armored Brigade* led by their commander, Colonel Uri Orr. A fierce armored battle ensued between the lead elements of Colonel Orr's brigade and the 91st Armored Brigade of the 1st Armored Division. This battle swirled around the Nafekh camp during the remaining hours of daylight, but by nightfall the position was securely in Israeli hands.[70]

When the battle around Lieutenant Zwicka ceased around 1700 hours, he found himself standing in the turret of his fifth or sixth Centurion, suddenly unable to make a decision as to what to do next. MAJ Dov, who was now the nominal *188th Armored Brigade* commander, rushed up to greet Lieutenant Zwicka. As he fought an overwhelming lethargy, Lieutenant Zwicka painfully climbed out of the turret and dropped to the ground, where he stated, "I can't anymore." MAJ Dov did not say a word; he just hugged Lieutenant Zwicka and led him to the medical evacuation center.[71] There is no way to calculate the damage that this iron-willed lieutenant inflicted upon the Syrian Army's plan while leading a small, ad hoc force of repaired Centurion tanks.

As it grew dark on the second night of battle the situation had started to improve for the Israelis who were beginning to turn the tide on the Golan Heights. In the north *7th Armored Brigade* continued its stubborn defense along the tank ditch with its 35 Centurion tanks between the *77th* and *74th Armored Battalions*. In the south Major General Laner had taken command and had sixty tanks, including the twelve that remained of the *188th Armored Brigade*, stretching from Kuneitra on the *7th Armored Brigade's* southern flank to the Arik Bridge.

The Initiative Starts to Shift

In the north, the Syrians prepared the 81st Tank Brigade from the General Headquarters Reserve to continue the attack. At 2200 hours, the 81st Tank Brigade crossed through the widened breach lanes in the Israeli tank ditch and dashed uphill into the awaiting tanks of the *77th Armored Battalion*. In the darkness, the Israeli's heard the tanks coming but could not engage them with long-range fire. When the enemy tanks were finally close enough to shoot, there were simply too many to destroy before they overran the defense. In the confusion, a Syrian tank battalion was able to penetrate the defense unhindered, and sped towards the rear of the Israeli positions.[72] Though the remnants of the *74th* and *77th Armored Battalions* continued to fight, a marauding enemy tank battalion in the Israeli rear made collapse of the defense seem imminent.

Colonel Ben-Gal had patiently waited to commit his reserve tank company until the crucial moment when it looked as if his defense might collapse. When he transferred the *82nd Armored Battalion* to the *Barak Brigade* before the battle began, he wisely retained control of one of the tank companies, which he used to constitute his reserve. Colonel Ben-Gal specifically chose this company from among those of his brigade because of the reputation of the company commander, Captain Meir "Tiger" Zamir.[73] At age twenty-six Captain Zamir was widely regarded as the best and fiercest tank commander in the brigade and would live up to that standing during the next thirty-six hours of fighting.

Colonel Ben-Gal gave Captain Zamir broad guidance to destroy enemy forces that had broken through the defense. He realized that his company of nine Centurions would confront a battalion of thirty to thirty-five T-55s in the dark, giving the Syrians a tremendous edge. Thus, instead of rushing headlong into the battle against an enemy force that had the advantage of night vision equipment, Captain Zamir wisely decided to let the Syrian tanks come to him where the Israeli tanks could even the odds by picking concealed positions. He decided to position his company in an ambush over watching the Dan Road, assuming that the Syrians would choose this high-speed avenue of approach. One group of four tanks under the command of his executive officer would illuminate the Syrian tanks with searchlights once they entered the ambush. The remaining five tanks under his direct control would then open fire.[74] With the ambush in position, Captain Zamir directed his company to shut off its engines and wait in absolute silence for the arrival of the Syrian tank battalion.

The long column of Syrian tanks drove down the road exactly as expected, but there were more Syrian tanks than the ambush line could cover. Captain Zamir decided to let the first part of the column pass and engage the last half first. He patiently waited until the last tank of the column entered the kill zone before giving the order to initiate fire. He was keenly aware that to trigger the ambush early would allow tanks not yet in the kill zone to maneuver on his positions. However, tanks that passed through the kill zone might not realize that the vehicles behind them were no longer following. Therefore, Captain Zamir assumed the risk of letting approximately twenty tanks exit the engagement area before triggering the ambush. When the executive officer turned on the searchlights, Zamir's five tanks immediately opened fire. Flames from burning Syrian tanks further illuminated the kill zone, and in a matter of a few minutes, fifteen T-55s sat smoldering along the road. With his entire company still intact, Zamir moved his tanks back parallel along the road in order to catch the first twenty tanks that unknowingly escaped the ambush. Though it took several hours of searching, he finally located the remaining tanks and destroyed them all in a similar ambush. The audacious exploits of "Tiger" Zamir had destroyed an entire Syrian tank battalion at the cost of three Centurion tanks.[75] With the success of the second ambush, it looked like the Israeli defense would hold.

While Captain Zamir's company destroyed the Syrian tanks that had broken through, Kahalani's tanks destroyed the others still in the area of the defensive. In tank on tank combat it looked as if the Syrians were simply no match for the great skill and resolute persistence of the Israeli tank crews. With the fight ending around 0200 hours, Lieutenant Colonel Kahalani set out to consolidate and reorganize his battalion of eleven tanks into two groups under the control of his only two surviving company commanders. Next, he organized the rearming and refueling of the tanks while establishing a security plan to protect against marauding Syrian antitank teams.[76] Though heavily attrited, thanks to Lieutenant Colonel Kahalani's leadership, the *77th Armored Battalion* would be ready to fight again in the morning.

Lieutenant Colonel Nofshe's *74th Armored Battalion* had a much easier fight this night. He personally orchestrated his unit's defense, making his gunners hold their fire until the Syrians were just 450 meters away. In less than ten minutes the Syrian attack was defeated and thirty T-62s were burning in front of the Israeli defensive positions. Nofshe's unit destroyed an entire Syrian tank battalion without the loss of a single tank. The Syrians continued to harass the *7th Armored Brigade* positions throughout the night but did not renew their attack.[77] In this particular engagement, the commander's presence on the battlefield proved decisive. By patiently waiting to engage the Syrian tanks at close range, Lieutenant Colonel Nofshe allowed the Israeli gunners to negate the Syrian advantage of night vision. Had they initiated fire too soon, the Syrians could have engaged him from a distance that his gunners could not have observed or they might have used the darkness to envelop his depleted force from a flank. However, at 450 meters, the engagement was over before the Syrian gunners realized what was happening and could return accurate fire.

At first light on the eighth of October, Colonel Ben-Gal drove forward to meet with his subordinates. Accompanying Lieutenant Colonel Kahalani on a tour of his positions, Ben-Gal counted the hulks of 130 Syrian tanks in front of the *77th Armored Battalion's* defense. Colonel Ben-Gal was astonished at the destruction wrought by the tank commanders of his unit. However, he knew that the Syrian attack was not over, and that the first Israeli reserves arriving continued to go to the southern sector of the Golan Heights. Before leaving, Colonel Ben-Gal emphasized the need to hold out for at least another twenty-four hours. By that time, the Israeli *679th Armored Brigade* would be ready to counterattack.[78] The knowledge that reinforcements would arrive shortly was quick to rejuvenate the tank crews' motivation to continue fighting.

Meanwhile, the Syrians were astonished at how quickly five of their tank and mechanized brigades had vanquished, not knowing that a single Israeli armored brigade was responsible for that destruction. In spite of the continued failure and heavy losses, the commander of the Syrian 7th Infantry Division, Brigadier General Omar Abrash, a graduate of the U.S. Army Command and General Staff College, received orders from Syrian General Headquarters to continue the attack.[79] The Syrian 7th Infantry Division was close to complete exhaustion but General Abrash pressed the attack with company- and battalion-sized elements throughout the eighth of October. Though these piecemeal attacks were unsuccessful in gaining ground, they did further attrit the Israeli defenders and drained their supply of ammunition. He planned to commit his second echelon to the fight that night but shortly before this attack was to begin his tank was hit and burst into flames, killing the Syrian Army's best commander. With the death of its division commander the 7th Infantry Division's attack was postponed until morning.[80]

By the end of the day, Colonel Ben-Gal's entire defense consisted of just twenty-one tanks; eight under Lieutenant Colonel Nofshe, seven with Lieutenant Colonel Kahalani, and Captain Zamir's six-tank reserve.[81] Despite the heavy attrition, the *7th Armored Brigade* was still strongly determined to hold their positions.

By the morning of the eighth of October, the Israelis were beginning to seize the initiative in the central and southern portions of the Golan Heights. Now the reserves were flowing into the area in ever growing numbers and the commanders began reorganizing the front to push the Syrian's armor back over the Purple Line. Colonel

Orr's brigade, now attached to Brigadier General Eitan's *36th Armored Infantry Division*, was driving east toward Ein Zivan, Tel Hazeika and Ramtania. This movement was paralleled by Colonel Sarig's *17th Armored Brigade* of Major General Laner's *240th Armored Division* moving through Kuzabia and across the Tap Line Road toward Hushniyah. Joining this offensive in the south were the three brigades of Major General Moshe Peled's *146th Armored Division* moving toward the Gamla Rise and El Al.[82]

The attack by Major General Laner's left and Brigadier General Peled's right now threatened the overextended Syrian 5th Infantry Division with a double envelopment. The 5th Division's commander, Brigadier General Ali Aslan, realized he had no reserve forces to counter either of the envelopment threats and began withdrawing to establish a new defensive line across the southern Golan Heights. At about the same time the commander of the Syrian 1st Armored Division, Colonel Tewfiq Juhni, committed his last remaining tanks in an effort to capture Nafekh. Once more an intense tank battle swirled around and along the roads in the central Golan Heights but the Israelis would not relinquish the initiative they had gained.[83]

By evening in the southern Golan Heights Lieutenant Colonel Orr's brigade securely held Sindiana, Colonel Sarig's brigade had reached the Tap Line Road west of Hushniyah and the leading brigades of Brigadier General Peled's division had recaptured Ramat Magshimim.[84]

The Ninth and Tenth of October--Back to the Purple Line

Major General Chakour realized continued assaults against the high ground in the north between the Hermonit and the Booster were destined for failure. The Israeli *74th Armored Battalion* continually repulsed these attacks across the steep, open ground before they even reached the Israeli defensive positions. However, attacks through the rock-strewn, broken ground of the Kuneitra Gap just south of the Booster had garnered more success over the previous forty-eight hours. The heavily attrited Syrian 7th Infantry Division made its final assault with the reinforced 121st Mechanized Brigade in an attempt to break the Israeli line in this area.[85] Standing between the 7th Infantry Division and success were the seven tanks of Lieutenant Colonel Kahalani's *77th Armored Battalion*.

Lieutenant Colonel Kahalani knew that his tiny force of seven tanks could not hold the ground that his battalion had defended against the better part of a brigade. Instead, he meticulously bounded his tanks back one at a time, constantly sniping at the advancing Syrians as he gave ground. While the Syrian attack continued, Lieutenant Colonel Kahalani's tactics greatly slowed their advance. After two hours of fighting, the Syrian attack had only gained around two thousand meters.[86] However, while the Syrian attack was slow, it was still gaining ground on the remainder of the *77th Armored Battalion*. Colonel Ben-Gal understood that Lieutenant Colonel Kahalani could not delay the Syrian attack indefinitely, so again he wisely committed his reserve at just the right time.

Instead of attacking the enemy head on, Captain Zamir shrewdly chose to maneuver his company south down the Heights to a position along the enemy's flank. Once in place, he led the charge of his tanks directly into the flank of the Syrian attack. The shock effect and surprise of "Tiger" Zamir's daring assault broke the spirit of the Syrian advance. The Syrian 121st Mechanized Brigade's attack turned into a disorganized retreat.[87] Captain Zamir's exploits clearly prove that a well led, small, motivated, and determined force can defeat a larger foe. In this example, a company of just six tanks defeated the remnants of a brigade primarily because of the bold and audacious actions of its commander. Furthermore, Zamir led the attack into the flank of this numerically superior force from the front, setting a personal example of fearlessness for his men. Once more, leadership decided the outcome of a battle.

Although Captain Zamir's daring exploits repulsed the Syrian attack, the *7th Armored Brigade's* position was still tenuous at best. The brigade mustered only twenty-one tanks, while the Syrians still had the uncommitted 70th Republican Guard Armored Brigade from the Syrian General Headquarters Forces; composed of Soviet-made T-62 tanks and BMP armored personnel carriers. Though Israeli mechanics worked through the night to repair damaged tanks at the brigade's maintenance collection point, none of these vehicles would be combat ready for at least another few hours.[88]

Major General Chakour knew that time was running out and if he did not seize the Golan Heights in the next twelve hours the Israeli reserves would arrive. Using the cover of darkness, Colonel Rifat Assad's 70th Republican Guard Tank Brigade moved forward and attacked through the breach lanes in the tank ditch. Like the previous attempts, a massive artillery and rocket barrage preceded the attack. Immediately following the artillery bombardment, ground attack aircraft made numerous strikes on Israeli positions and Soviet-made Mi-8 Hip helicopters dropped anti-armor hunter-killer teams behind the Israeli lines. The Israeli Air Force intercepted this helicopter force destroying several in the air and then assisted in the destruction of several teams on the ground.[89]

The garrison of Bunker 107 was the first to spot the Syrian advance. With the sound of panic in his voice, one of the soldiers shouted that there were fifty Syrian tanks approaching his position. The platoon leader, Lieutenant Avraham Elimelech, broke the tension when he calmly replied, "So what? There are fifty more approaching mine." Lieutenant Colonel Kahalani's *77th Battalion* faced over one hundred T-62 tanks moving on his position. Rather than stay in position and face certain death, he requested permission from the brigade commander to withdraw. Colonel Ben-Gal immediately approved the retreat.[90]

The lead elements of the Syrian attack arrived just as Lieutenant Colonel Kahalani finished positioning his forces along the road just west of Kuneitra. A close range tank duel ensued with the *77th Armored Battalion* on the verge of destruction. With the defense on the brink of collapse, Colonel Ben-Gal once again committed his reserve to hold the line. Captain Zamir led his force of six Centurions forward, this time crashing headlong into the Syrian attack. While he was able to destroy numerous Syrian tanks, his unit ran out of ammunition before stopping the Syrian attack. Requesting permission to withdraw long enough to rearm, Colonel Ben-Gal instead ordered him to hold his position, because "Maybe the *sight* of Jewish tanks will frighten them off."[91] The situation was more desperate than ever before, but Colonel Ben-Gal knew reinforcements were very close to arriving on the scene. He knew that his last remaining tanks need only hold out for a little while longer.

Seeing no other recourse, Colonel Ben-Gal ordered Kahalani to counterattack into the advancing Syrians. Lieutenant Colonel Kahalani now augmented with an additional tank platoon straight from the brigade's repair shop saw just one chance for survival. The Syrians were advancing in two wings, and if he could counterattack between them, he might be able to break their cohesion. As he looked out onto the battlefield, he knew it would take great courage to lead a counterattack against so many Syrian tanks. Nevertheless, without any further thought, he led the advance of his tanks between the Syrian columns. As soon as he jumped off, Lieutenant Colonel Kahalani came face to face with four Syrian T-62s. Within ninety seconds, his gunner destroyed all four Syrian tanks.[92] Lieutenant Colonel Kahalani's force cleverly maneuvered through the broken ground separating the Syrian thrusts, carefully choosing positions where it was very difficult for the Syrians to engage them. While the Syrians had trouble engaging his force, Lieutenant Colonel Kahalani's tanks continued to attrit Syrian tanks in the two advancing ranks.[93] The sudden appearance of Israeli tanks intermingled with their own forces started to cause confusion and panic in the Syrian ranks.

The tide of the battle turned with the arrival of Lieutenant Colonel Yossi Ben Hanan leading a motley crew of thirteen Centurions. Lieutenant Colonel Ben Hanan, previously a battalion commander in the *Barak Brigade*, was outside of the country on his honeymoon when the war started. Upon return to Israel, he conferred with Israeli Defense Force Headquarters before driving to the Golan Heights. With instructions from Major General Hofi, he went to the Northern Front's maintenance collection point, where he assembled thirteen damaged but operable Centurions. He then quickly organized tank crews out of the wounded and newly arrived reservists. Realizing how grave the situation was, he immediately led this ad hoc force into battle.[94]

Lieutenant Colonel Ben Hanan's force arrived at the crucial point in the battle. The Syrian attack was still strong, but Lieutenant Colonel Kahalani's counterattack caused it to falter, even though he was down to just three tanks. Lieutenant Colonel Hanan maneuvered his tanks to the Booster, joining the four remaining tanks of the *74th*

Armored Battalion, placing him on the flank of the Syrian forces. He immediately launched a counterattack into the Syrian flank. Within seconds, twenty-two Syrian tanks were burning. The ferocity of Lieutenant Colonel Hanan's assault broke the Syrian advance. The arrival of additional Centurions made the Syrians think the Israeli reserves had arrived and were launching a major counterattack. The Syrian attack quickly turned into a rout, with Syrian tank crews abandoning their vehicles and fleeing back towards Syria on foot.[95] The gallant attack of Lieutenant Colonel Hanan's piecemeal force had broken the "Pride of the Syrian Army;" the renowned 70th Republican Guards Tank Brigade.

Captain "Tiger" Zamir's Centurion was the only tank in his command that was able to move back to the resupply point near Nafekh under its own power. With the arrival of reinforcements he was now able to take a well-deserved rest and rebuild his decimated company. He and his newly rebuilt company would play a key role in the Israeli counteroffensive into Syria that was to come on the eleventh of October.[96]

The battle ended with only seven operational tanks in the *7th Armored Brigade*, three with Lieutenant Colonel Kahalani and four with Lieutenant Colonel Nofshe. However, the brigade had destroyed the majority of two Syrian divisions. The charred hulks of over 500 Syrian vehicles littered across the northern Golan gave grim testimony to this fact. With such extensive destruction in the area between Tel-Hermonit and the Booster, the Israelis named the pass "The Valley of Tears."[97] The *7th Armored Brigade* had won a decisive victory against seemingly overwhelming odds, at the steep cost of ninety-eight of its own tanks.

Throughout the day in the south the *20th* and *14th Armored Brigades* of the IDF's *146th Armored Division* continued to attack, pushing the battered Syrian 47th Armored Brigade back toward the Purple Line. These forces completed the encirclement and destruction of the 47th Armored Brigade near Juhader. The Israeli brigades then turned their attention toward pushing the remaining forces of the 5th Infantry Division back across the Purple Line. Moving along another road, the *19th Armored Brigade* of the *146th Armored Division* pushed inland against the main enemy concentrations near the Hushniyah camp. Facing the remnants of two armored brigades, the *146th Armored Brigade* fought a fierce battle. With the assistance of the *679th Armored Brigade* from the north, the Israeli brigades boxed in the Syrians. The 1st Syrian Armored Division realized its plight and tried in vain to extricate its forces from the encirclement. However, the fate of the 1st Armored Division was sealed during the day with only minute remnants escaping and making their way back behind Syrian lines.[98]

On Wednesday, the tenth of October, all three of the Israeli divisions on the Golan Heights continued to press slowly forward. By the evening the Israelis had driven the Syrians back to the post-1967 ceasefire line, erasing all of their gains over the previous four days. Moreover, the Israelis had devastated the Syrian army in the process. The Syrian units that did manage to make it back from the Golan Heights were demoralized and disorganized. They had suffered terrible losses and were in no shape to counter the Israeli counteroffensive that began on the eleventh of October.[99]

In the battles on the Golan Heights alone, the Syrians lost 1,150 main battle tanks, 3,500 soldiers were killed in battle, with about another 10,000 wounded in action and 370 taken prisoner by the Israelis. The Israelis lost 250 Centurions hit badly enough to be considered "knocked out;" however, 152 of those were repaired and eventually returned to battle by the Israeli ordnance men. The Israelis lost 772 soldiers killed in action, 2,453 wounded, and 65 had been taken prisoner.[100]

The Israeli success on the Golan Heights was primarily due to the human factor. It was that outstanding Israeli small-unit leadership that developed units with strong combat motivation, high morale, and subordinate leaders capable of taking daring and decisive action that allowed the Israelis victory against overwhelming odds. Israeli leadership was undoubtedly the decisive factor in the battle. Despite what appeared to be insurmountable odds, the Israelis determinedly remained in their positions and engaged the advancing masses of Syrian armor for three straight days. The use of numerous bold counterattacks and the timely commitment of reserve forces stole the initiative from the Syrians. On several occasions the daring exploits of brave leaders completely changed the course of the battle. Additionally, the fearlessness of the Israeli tank commanders rallied their soldiers and prevented panic, even when defeat seemed imminent. The leaders continued heroism had convinced their soldiers that they would accomplish their mission regardless of the situation.

---

[1]Samuel M. Katz, *Israeli Tank Battles: Yom Kippur to Lebanon* (London: Arms and Armor Press, 1988), 12.

[2]Kenneth M. Pollack, *Arabs At War: Military Effectiveness, 1948-1991* (Lincoln: University of Nebraska Press, 2002), 484.

[3]Jerry Asher, and Eric Hammel, *Duel For The Golan: The 100-Hour Battle That Saved Israel* (New York: William Morrow and Company, Inc., 1987), 83.

[4]Ibid., 84.

[5]Gary Rashba, "Sacrificial Stand in the Golan Heights," *Military History Magazine*, 1 October 1998, 3.

[6]Jac Weller, "Middle East Tank Killers," *Royal United Services Institute Journal* (December 1974): 17.

[7]Asher and Hammel, *Duel for the Golan,* 84.

[8]Rashba, "Sacrificial Stand in the Golan Heights," 3.

[9]Asher and Hammel, *Duel for the Golan,* 93.

[10]Katz, *Israeli Tank Battles*, 31.

[11]Avigdor Kahalani, *The Heights of Courage: A Tank Leader's War on the Golan* (London: Greenwood Press, 1984), 37.

[12]Asher and Hammel, *Duel for the Golan,* 98.

[13]Ibid., 99.

[14]Ibid.

[15]Ibid., 100.

[16]Robin Trautman, "The Yom Kippur War," *The Jewish Student Online Research Center,* 1 [article on-line]; available from hhtp://campus.northpark.edu/history/WebChron/MiddleEast/ YomKippurWar.html; Internet.

[17]Asher and Hammel, *Duel for the Golan,* 101.

[18]Chaim Herzog, *The War of Atonement* (Boston: Boston: Little, Brown and Company, 1975), 78.

[19]Asher and Hammel, *Duel for the Golan,* 102.

[20]Ibid., 103.

[21]Herzog, *The War of Atonement,* 82.

[22]Rashba, "Sacrificial Stand in the Golan Heights," 5.

[23]Ibid., 6.

[24]Asher and Hammel, *Duel for the Golan,* 104.

[25]Rashba, "Sacrificial Stand in the Golan Heights," 6.

[26]David Eshel, *Chariots of the Desert: The Story of the Israeli Armoured Corps* (London: Brassey's Defence Publishers, 1989), 95.

[27] Herzog, *The War of Atonement*, 88.

[28] Trevor N. Dupuy, *Elusive Victory: The Arab-Israeli Wars, 1947-1974* (Fairfax: Hero Books, 1984), 441.

[29] Herzog, *The War of Atonement*, 89.

[30] Katz, *Israeli Tank Battles*, 41.

[31] Kahalani, *The Heights of Courage*, 43.

[32] Herzog, *The War of Atonement*, 92.

[33] Asher and Hammel, *Duel for the Golan*, 108.

[34] Ibid., 117.

[35] Ibid.

[36] Ibid., 118.

[37] Dupuy, *Elusive Victory*, 444.

[38] Herzog, *The War of Atonement*, 95.

[39] Eshel, *Chariots of the Desert*, 102.

[40] Kahalani, *The Heights of Courage*, 44.

[41] Samuel M. Katz, *Fire & Steel: Israel's 7th Armored Brigade* (New York: Pocket Books, 1996), 145.

[42] Kahalani, *The Heights of Courage*, 46.

[43] Ibid., 53.

[44] Dupuy, *Elusive Victory*, 489.

[45] Kahalani, *The Heights of Courage*, 58.

[46] Pollack, *Arabs At War*, 488.

[47] Dupuy, *Elusive Victory*, 493.

[48] Herzog, *The War of Atonement*, 104.

[49] Asher and Hammel, *Duel for the Golan*, 128.

[50] Eshel, *Chariots of the Desert,* 108.

[51] Asher and Hammel, *Duel for the Golan,* 130.

[52] Ibid., 132.

[53] Eshel, *Chariots of the Desert,* 112.

[54] Pollack, *Arabs At War,* 496.

[55] Katz, *Fire & Steel,* 154.

[56] Kahalani, *The Heights of Courage,* 65.

[57] Ibid.

[58] Ibid., 67

[59] Pollack, *Arabs At War,* 499.

[60] Herzog, *The War of Atonement,* 108.

[61] Raful Eitan, *A Soldier's Story: The Life and Times of an Israeli War Hero* (New York: Shapolsky Publishers, Inc., 1991), 152.

[62] Eshel, *Chariots of the Desert,* 115.

[63] Asher and Hammel, *Duel for the Golan,* 154.

[64] Eshel, *Chariots of the Desert,* 118.

[65] Dupuy, *Elusive Victory,* 498.

[66] Asher and Hammel, *Duel for the Golan,* 156.

[67] Herzog, *The War of Atonement,* 115.

[68] Eshel, *Chariots of the Desert,* 120.

[69] Dupuy, *Elusive Victory,* 502.

[70] Eitan, *A Soldier's Story,* 154.

[71] Herzog, *The War of Atonement,* 116.

[72] Kahalani, *The Heights of Courage,* 78.

[73] Asher and Hammel, *Duel for the Golan,* 160.

[74] Ibid., 162.

[75] Dupuy, *Elusive Victory*, 505.

[76] Kahalani, *The Heights of Courage*, 79.

[77] Asher and Hammel, *Duel for the Golan*, 168.

[78] Kahalani, *The Heights of Courage*, 84.

[79] Pollack, *Arabs At War*, 502.

[80] Dupuy, *Elusive Victory*, 510.

[81] Kahalani, *The Heights of Courage*, 92.

[82] Asher and Hammel, *Duel for the Golan*, 200.

[83] Pollack, *Arabs At War*, 505.

[84] Dupuy, *Elusive Victory*, 512.

[85] Pollack, *Arabs At War*, 506.

[86] Kahalani, *The Heights of Courage*, 95.

[87] Asher and Hammel, *Duel for the Golan*, 202.

[88] Kahalani, *The Heights of Courage*, 97.

[89] Herzog, *The War of Atonement*, 118.

[90] Asher and Hammel, *Duel for the Golan*, 204

[91] Kahalani, *The Heights of Courage*, 101.

[92] Ibid., 102.

[93] Asher and Hammel, *Duel for the Golan*, 206.

[94] Ibid., 207.

[95] Ibid., 208.

[96] Ibid., 238.

[97] Herzog, *The War of Atonement*, 124.

[98] Eshel, *Chariots of the Desert,* 122.

[99] Pollack, *Arabs At War,* 508.

[100] Asher and Hammel, *Duel for the Golan,* 272.

CHAPTER 3

ISRAELI LEADERSHIP

During the October 1973 Yom Kippur War, a massive Soviet-style Syrian Army suffered a crushing defeat at the hands of a greatly outnumbered Israeli Defense Force on the Golan Heights. While the sheer number of attacking Syrian forces nearly overwhelmed the Israeli defenses, Israeli tank commanders acted with great courage and conviction and turned the tide of the battle. Therefore, Israeli small-unit leadership was the decisive factor in the battle of the Golan Heights. To fully support this argument, in this chapter I will first define military leadership and show that leadership can be a decisive factor in a battle. Second, I will discuss General Orde Charles Wingate's Leadership Principles that the Israeli Defense Force is built upon. Third, I will show how following General Wingate's Leadership Principles made the difference at the small-unit level for the Israelis. Last, I will explain how the IDF selects and trains its small-unit leaders. This approach should prove conclusively that competent and confident Israeli small-unit leadership was the decisive aspect of this battle.

Leadership Defined and Israeli Doctrine

Leadership can be an important cause of victory or defeat on the battlefield. The 2002 edition of the U.S. Army's Field Manual 3-0, *Operations*, defines a unit's ability to fight as *combat power*. An element's combat power is determined by "combining the effects of maneuver, firepower, protection, information and leadership."[1] Of these five aspects of combat power, leadership is the most essential dynamic. Leaders are the ones who inspire their soldiers with the will to win and provide them with purpose, direction, and motivation. Leaders also influence the fight with their personal presence on the battlefield and by displaying courage and conviction in the face of the enemy.[2] Therefore, when opposing forces are nearly equal, the quality of a unit's leadership can provide the decisive edge in combat. Byzantine Emperor Heraclius (c. 575-641) fully understood the importance of leadership in battle. He was a brilliant and resourceful general who was considered a talented strategist and tactician. He fought in many battles and fully understood the importance of leadership at the small-unit level when he said,

> Of every one-hundred men,
> Ten shouldn't even be there,
> Eighty are nothing but targets,
> Nine are real fighters...
> We are lucky to have them,
> They make the battle.
> Ah, but one,
> One of them is a warrior, a real leader,
> ...he will bring the others back.[3]

Leadership can provide a decisive advantage even when an army is greatly outnumbered. The 1999 edition of the U.S. Army Field Manual 22-10, *Military Leadership,* states, "Competent and confident leaders who are bold, innovative, and willing to take well-calculated risks can overcome enemies that outnumber them."[4] Thus, a small army with good leaders can quite often defeat a larger but poorly led army.

Even in modern, mechanized warfare, humans still decide the fate of battles. Despite the tremendous firepower of modern day tanks, armored personnel carriers, and artillery pieces, leaders are still required to provide purpose, direction, and motivation to the soldiers who operate these weapons systems. Therefore, a skilled leader of a small unit who can effectively organize his soldiers to fight as a cohesive team can defeat a larger force that is relying on its sheer mass to win. General George S. Patton Jr. truly believed that leadership at the small-unit level was the decisive aspect of battle. He constantly reminded his officers "Wars may be fought with weapons, but they are won by men. It is the spirit of the men who follow and the man who leads that gains the victory."[5]

Without strong leadership at the small-unit level, larger forces do have obvious advantages over smaller ones. History has shown that for units that are poorly led the sight of a larger force taking the field can trigger panic in the smaller force resulting in a subsequent disorganized retreat or even rout. However, as the Israelis showed during the battle for the Golan Heights a well-led unit will stand and face a larger enemy, especially if the leaders "set a personal example of fearlessness."[6] Leading and fighting by example, through bold and daring actions and by means of being present on the ground where the fighting is heaviest, a commander can rally his troops in front of overwhelming odds, prevent panic and gain a decisive victory. Furthermore, in a unit trained to fight as a cohesive team, soldiers are more willing to fight because the team provides mutual support that suppresses fear. The soldiers see themselves fighting as a member of a team, not as individuals. Therefore, a small, cohesive unit that is motivated and determined can defeat a larger foe.

To compensate for the IDFs small size, the Israeli military trains its leaders in an unconventional method. The training emphasizes individual responsibility, leaders' freedom of action, group morale, cohesion, inventive tactics, and daring leadership.[7] The IDF feels that these are the necessary skills needed to allow their leaders to be successful on a battlefield where the enemy has a numerical advantage.

Israeli military doctrine calls for the IDF to achieve quick success on the battlefield. Even when greatly outnumbered, small-unit leaders must possess the flexibility and freedom to use their own initiative in order to capitalize upon any tactical advantage. The Israeli military ensures that its principles and its training fosters these characteristics down to the lowest levels making speed, the offense, initiative, and improvisation hallmarks of the Israeli military ethos.[8]

The IDF doctrine states that all officers must possess common or basic values. These values are what allow Israeli soldiers to believe in their officers and allow those officers to lead in the manner that has led to the survival of a nation surrounded by enemies. U.S. Representative Dan Daniels (speaking about the U.S. military) explained the reason behind and the importance of these same values during the hearings on the Beirut tragedy:

> When an officer accepts command of troops, he accepts not only the responsibility of accomplishing a mission, but the guardianship of those who serve under his command. The military hierarchy exists and can function because enlisted personnel entrust their well-being and their lives to those with command authority. When those in command authority either abdicate that authority or neglect that guardianship, more is lost than lives. Lost also is the trust that enables those who follow to follow those who lead.

The IDF realize the importance of this and has developed ten basic values that will allow commanders to accomplish their mission while at the same time ensure that the military hierarchy exists and can function. These ten basic values are:

- **Tenacity of Purpose in Performing Missions and Drive to Victory** – The IDF officer will fight and conduct himself with courage in the face of all dangers and obstacles. He will persevere in his missions resolutely and thoughtfully even to the point of endangering his life.

- **Responsibility** – The IDF officer will see himself as an active participant in the defense of the state, its citizens and residents. He will carry out his duties at all times with initiative, involvement and diligence with common sense and within the framework of his authority, while prepared to bear responsibility for his conduct.

- **Credibility** – The IDF officer shall present things objectively, completely and precisely, in planning, performing and reporting. He will act in such a manner that his peers and commanders can rely upon him in performing his tasks.
- **Personal Example** – The IDF officer will comport himself as required and will demand of himself no less than he demands of his soldiers, out of recognition of his ability and responsibility to serve as a role model.
- **Human Life** – During combat the IDF officer will endanger himself and his soldiers only to the extent required to carry out the mission.
- **Purity of Arms** – The IDF officer will use his weapons and force only for the purpose of the mission, only to the extent necessary and will maintain his humanity even during combat.
- **Professionalism** – The IDF officer will acquire the professional knowledge and skills required to perform his tasks, and will implement them while striving continuously to perfect his personal and the units' collective achievements.
- **Discipline** – The IDF officer will strive to the best of his ability to fully and successfully complete all that is required of him according to orders.
- **Comradeship** – The IDF officer will act out of fraternity and devotion to his soldiers, and will always go to their assistance when they need his help despite any danger or difficulty, even to the point of risking his own life.
- **Sense of Mission** – The IDF officer will view his service in the IDF as a mission. He will be ready to give his all, including his life, in order to defend the state, its citizens and residents.[9]

The IDF realizes that in the end it is the commanders who must inspire their soldiers to win, and provide them with a clear purpose, direction, and motivation. By displaying courage and fearlessness on the battlefield in the face of overwhelming odds and seeming defeat, a commander can rally his troops together and achieve victory. These vital elements of effective tactical leadership at the small-unit level are clearly illustrated during the battle of the Golan Heights during the 1973 Yom Kippur War.

Principles of Israeli Small-Unit Leadership

The IDF was born in battle in 1948 with the creation of the nation of Israel. This newly born IDF compensated for its initial deficiencies in numbers, weaponry, and training by selecting leaders who possessed dedication and motivation, intelligence and improvisation. These traits eventually came to personify the Israeli officer and grew into the fundamental characteristics of decisiveness, purposefulness, leadership by personal example, utilization of night warfare and surprise attacks, and the ability to improvise.[10]

Moshe Dayan was one of these initial officers and when he became the IDFs Chief of Staff in 1953 he insisted on officers who were fighting leaders rather than managers in uniforms. He institutionalized the concept that "Officers do not send their men into battle; they lead them into battle."[11] His influence is still present in today's Israeli officer corps.

At the tactical level the Israeli Defense Force has adopted General Orde Charles Wingate's Principles of Leadership as the basis of their leadership doctrine. General Wingate was born at Naini Tal, India on 26 February 1903, the son of a deeply religious British army officer. He was educated at Charterhouse and the Royal Military Academy at Woolwich. He was commissioned 2d Lieutenant in the artillery in 1923 and served in Palestine during the Arab revolts from 1936 to 1939. He served as an advisor to the Jewish Settlement Police, where he helped the Jewish leaders create and train the Special Night Squads of the Haganah in guerrilla and counterinsurgency warfare.[12] These units later became the Palmach, which is the precursor to the modern day Israeli Defense Force. During those formative years the Jewish leaders were trained using General

Wingate's seven principles and they have left their mark on both the doctrine and tactics of the present day Israeli Defense Force.[13]

General Wingate's Principles of Leadership are simple and straightforward. These characteristic principles include: (1) leadership based on personal example, (2) purposeful yet meticulous discipline, always focused on the practical and operational aspects, (3) careful planning of any operation and the dissemination of the purpose of the plan to the lowest levels, (4) full delegation of authority to subordinate commanders allowing for improvisation in accordance with the changing conditions of battle, (5) concentration of forces on the major objective, while at the same time skillfully managing to fragment and scatter the forces when needed, (6) the exploitation of surprise, mobility and night maneuvers, and (7) the emphasis on the ideological motivation of the troops.[14] All seven of these principles are evident in the Israeli leadership at the tactical level during the battle for the Golan Heights during the 1973 Yom Kippur War.

General Wingate's principle of leading by personal example and from the front, is the motto preached the most during an Israeli officers training.[15] Moshe Dayan's "follow me" dictum has come to symbolize the Israeli officer corps. Israeli officers leading their soldiers into battle from the front was certainly the norm displayed during this battle. This is evident by the number of Israeli officers killed and wounded during the battle. At one point in the battle, during a lull in the fighting, Lieutenant Colonel Kahalani called his officers together for a face-to-face meeting to explain the situation and the upcoming battle plans. It was during this lull that he finally comprehended the number of leaders in his unit that had become casualties. He looked around at them and was shocked to realize that fewer than half of his original company and platoon commanders were still on the battlefield.[16] Officers at all levels of command were out fighting from the front in order to set an example for their soldiers. One must remember that the *188th Armored Brigade* commander, Colonel Ben-Shoham, was killed on the second day of fighting while engaging the lead elements of the Syrian 1st Armored Division along Tap Line Road in the southern sector of the Golan Heights. The Israeli enlisted soldiers and noncommissioned officers (NCOs) never had any doubt as to what was expected of them because their officers showed them by leading from the front. This is one of the key reasons that leadership played a decisive role in the battle.

According to General George S. Patton Jr., "Discipline must be a habit so ingrained that it is stronger than the excitement of battle or the fear of death. Discipline, which is but mutual trust and confidence, is the key to all success in war."[17] The IDF is a strong believer in the need for disciplined soldiers and units; however its discipline is focused more on operational and performance standards than on ceremonial details. The requirement is more for a clean rifle than for spit-shined boots. Soldiers are constantly disciplined to perform their duties within very tight time constraints; while a sharp uniform is not always essential, precise and timely performance is always demanded.[18] Lieutenant Colonel Kahalani recalls that on the ninth of October, three days into the battle on the Golan Heights, one of his company commanders saw a tank moving toward his position and because his unit was disciplined, the commander asked for permission to fire the opening shot of the battle. It was then that Lieutenant Colonel Kahalani realized that military discipline was one of the elements still binding his men together.[19] The discipline ingrained in the soldiers of the IDF by their leaders was stronger than the excitement of battle or the fear of death. The units and individuals had the courage to hold their positions even when they knew it meant certain death.

Careful planning of an operation and the dissemination of the purpose of the plan to the lowest levels are essential aspect of the IDF for two reasons. First, the IDF demands that small-unit leaders at all levels use their own initiative to make decisions on the battlefield, even if these decisions contradict the plan developed by their higher headquarters.[20] The IDF understands that small-unit commanders leading from the front who know the purpose of an operation, and have the flexibility and freedom to make decisions on the battlefield, are essential to the exploitation of success. This can only occur if everyone understands what is to be accomplished and why. Second, since Israeli officers lead from the front they incur a high casualty rate in every war; the Yom Kippur War was no different. The Israeli Army suffered 2,521 soldiers killed in action on both fronts during the war. Of those killed 606 or 24 percent were officers, including twenty-five Colonels and Lieutenant Colonels and over eighty majors.[21] One consequence of a high officer casualty rate is that NCOs had to step up to take command of platoons and companies. That this was able to occur in the middle of a desperate battle can be directly related to this Israeli leadership principle and is yet another reason that leadership was the decisive factor in the battle.

Because Israeli small-unit commanders lead from the front, they have the best picture of what is happening on the battlefield; therefore, they are obligated to use their own initiative to improvise in accordance with the changing conditions of battle. I had a chance to interview Lieutenant Colonel Eytan Yitshak, who was the Israeli Defense Force officer attending the U.S. Army Command and General Staff College in 2002, and we discussed this very point. He told me, "It is the duty of the officer on the ground to use his own initiative during battle to take advantage of an unexpected tactical advantage, even if it means disobeying orders from a superior officer."[22] Perfect examples of the use of this principle in the battle were the ambushes executed by both Lieutenant Zwicka and Captain "Tiger" Zamir. They were both ordered to conduct counterattacks but used their own initiative to set up ambushes instead because it better suited the tactical situation.

Every army tries to adhere to the principle of concentrating forces on the major objective, while at the same time skillfully managing to fragment and scatter the forces when needed. This principle is especially important for the Israeli Army because of its need to fight against a numerically superior enemy and on more than one front. After taking over command, Brigadier General Eitan immediately recognized that the most vital sector of the Golan Heights was the northern sector. He determined that this sector must be held at all costs because if lost to the Syrians it would be very difficult and costly in lives to recapture. He therefore placed his best unit, the *7th Armored Brigade*, in command of this decisive terrain.[23] In addition, brigade and battalion commanders were free to make their own decisions about where the bulk of their forces were needed while at the same time keeping back a reserve of some size to deal with unforeseen circumstances.

Since the IDF plans to fight in situations where they are outnumbered, they always plan for the exploitation of surprise, mobility, and night maneuvers to help make up for its lack in number.[24] In the 1973 Yom Kippur War the Arab coalition forces were just as mobile as the Israeli Army so neither side had an advantage over the other. The Arab coalition definitely had the advantage in night engagements because their Soviet-made tanks were equipped with night sights whereas the Israeli Centurions were not. The Arab coalition also had the advantage of choosing when the war would start and turned this into an element of strategic surprise, even if the surprise was not as complete as was hoped. Although the Arab coalition had the initial advantages in these areas, this did not prevent the Israelis from wrestling the initiative away from the Arabs, turning the tide of battle in their favor. The IDF tank commanders used their skills of improvisation to quickly overcome their disadvantage of not having night sights. They allowed the Syrian tanks to close within 500 meters and then used the Centurion tank's spotlights to light up their targets. On several occasions the Israeli commanders exploited surprise to stop Syrian assaults just when it looked like the Syrians were going to overrun the Israeli defenses. Two examples of this were the counterattacks executed on the ninth of October in the northern sector. The first was Lieutenant Colonel Kahalani's attack between the advancing Syrian columns of T-62 tanks and BMP Infantry Fighting Vehicles, which caused enough confusion to halt the advance even though the Israelis were greatly outnumbered. He bought enough time for Lieutenant Colonel Hanan's counterattack into the northern flank of this same Syrian formation with an ad hoc force scraped together from the units' maintenance collection point. These unexpected counterattacks surprised the Syrians and completely broke their spirit, causing their attack to fail.

    The IDF places a special emphasis on the ideological motivation of its troops. What makes soldiers stand and fight in the face of certain death when any reasonable man would turn and run? According to S. L. A. Marshall men do not fight for God, country or glory. They fight for the soldiers on their left and right--for their comrades in arms.[25] Although this is true even in the IDF, the Israeli soldiers also have another reason to fight. The history of the Jewish people has been one filled with oppression and massacre; from the Second Jewish Commonwealth being destroyed in A.D. 70 by the Roman Legions to the Holocaust at the hands of the Nazis in World War II.[26] The Israeli soldier therefore fights not only for his comrades, but also for the protection of his family, which is never far behind the fighting front. General George S. Patton Jr. once told his leaders "Defeat is not due to losses but to the destruction of the soul of the leaders."[27] The Israeli commanders also understand that a motivated soldier who has been imbued with the will to win is a potent force on the battlefield. As Lieutenant Colonel Kahalani said, "A strong will can overcome anything."[28] This desire to win was certainly evident in the Israeli units on the battlefields of the Golan Heights in 1973 and was yet another reason Israeli leadership was decisive.

Israeli Leadership Principles Put to Use at the Small-Unit Level

I have explained the Wingate principles that the Israeli leadership doctrine is based upon and have given examples of how each of these principles was put to use by the Israeli leadership during the battle for the Golan Heights in 1973. But how did the use of these leadership principles help produce a decisive victory at the tactical level? Adherence to these principles allowed the Israeli small-unit leaders to make timely decisions, rebuild cohesive combat crews and units during battle, and prevent panic in desperate situations.

Israeli commanders at the tactical level made many decisions at critical points in the fighting that turned the tide of battle to their favor. This was possible because leaders were leading from the front and had the authority to use their own initiative to make decisions without asking for permission to do so. The Israeli decision cycle was much faster than the centralized decision cycle the Arab small-unit leaders had to work under. The timely employment of Israeli reserve forces and reinforcements is a strong example. At critical times throughout the battle for the Golan Heights, an Israeli commander seemed to commit his last remaining reserve at just the precise moment needed. As replacements started to flow in, the Israeli commanders on the ground along the Purple Line were able to identify the locations on the battlefield that were under the most pressure and direct those forces, no matter how small, to the right place just in time to stave off disaster. This was possible because those commanders were out front where they could see the battlefield and size up the situation for themselves. It would not have been possible if the Israeli commanders had been tied to their command posts well behind the raging battle.

The Israeli combat experience of the Armor corps in previous wars demonstrated the importance of tank crew cohesion as a significant means of enduring sustained combat stresses.[29] This cohesion, certainly present in the beginning of the battle, suffered due to the large number of casualties and the Israeli commanders had to improvise during the battle to recreate it. Lieutenant Colonel Kahalani realized that he had to start rebuilding cohesion in his unit during the meeting he held with his leaders on the ninth of October. He opened this meeting with his commanders with this little speech: "Alright, friends, the battalion that you joined has high performance standards. During the last few days, we have been in a tough war. I want you to acclimatize quickly. Get to know your commanders and your crews--and become an organic part of the battalion."[30] Commanders all over the battlefield had to do the same thing as ad hoc formations made up of reconstituted crews and platoons began arriving from the units' tank repair shop.

The rebuilding of units is no easy task and is even that much more difficult in the middle of a desperate battle. However, the ability of the Israelis to accomplish this was a direct result of their small-unit leader's ability and turned out to be a decisive factor in the Israeli victory in the battle for the Golan Heights.

Combat on the modern battlefield is a brutal environment. The minute-to-minute life and death struggle can quickly take its toll on even the most seasoned combat soldiers. It is up to the leaders to prevent the breakdown of discipline in their units and prevent panic from setting in. The Israeli commanders realized that there were two ways to produce a calming effect on their soldiers. First was by letting their soldiers see them leading from the front and living under the same conditions as they were. In an interview with Captain Roger Cirillo after the Yom Kippur War retired General Aharon Davidi, the former head of the IDF Paratroopers, explained that when soldiers saw their leaders on the battlefield undergoing the same hardships as they were, it had a calming effect upon them. Therefore, it was important for commanders at all levels to be as close to the front as possible and visible to their troops, especially at critical times in the battle.[31] During lulls in the battle, Lieutenant Colonel Kahalani made it a point to walk around the tanks so his men could see him and he required his subordinate commanders to do the same. The second calming strategy was voice modulation over the radio during the battle. As the *77th Armored Battalion* began suffering casualties, Lieutenant Colonel Kahalani could not be where everyone in his battalion could see him but he realized that he could calm his soldiers by talking quietly and calmly while issuing crisp and simple orders on the radio.[32] Israeli soldiers did not panic, even during the most desperate situations, in combat because they saw their leaders fighting along side them and heard those leaders speaking calmly over the radio. Israeli leadership was decisive because it prevented a breakdown in that all-important commodity in combat--discipline.

A final way Israeli leadership was decisive on the battlefield was by leaders setting the example for their men during the heat of combat. As I have shown in this paper, the battle for the Golan Heights is full of situations where the tide of the battle turned because an Israeli commander led from the front and set a personal example for his men. As underscored by the former Prime Minister of Israel Yitzhak Rabin, "Leaders like Ben-Gal, Ben-Shoham, Kahalani and Eres did not send others to battle. Rather, they stood courageously at the head of the column and inspired their men to give more, even when they thought they had given their all. It was soldiers following leaders like these that won the battle of the Golan Heights and saved the nation of Israel."[33] Commanders like these were able to maintain their men's level of confidence, discipline and bravery by setting a personal example for them on the battlefield. Lieutenant Kahalani believes "You lead by example and gain respect by example,"[34] and the men of the *77th Armored Battalion* proved he was right on the battlefields of the Golan Heights in October of 1973.

I have shown that Israeli leadership at the small-unit level was the decisive factor in Israel's victory on the Golan Heights in the 1973 Yom Kippur War. The IDF believes that leadership in the one area where the Israeli Army will always hold an advantage over its enemies. To properly ensure this, Israel has developed its own unique way of selecting and training its leaders.

How The IDF Selects and Trains Its Leaders

When the U.N. created the nation of Israel in 1948 its citizens found themselves surrounded by hostile Arab nations, most of which rejected Israel's right to exist and many seeking to destroy the Jewish state. The Israeli War of Independence thus became a life and death struggle of an apocalyptic nature for the newly formed Jewish state. Israel quickly developed its own unique military culture as it fought for its survival.[35]

In addition to the life and death struggle for survival, the Israeli population also had a vivid memory of the Holocaust in World War II. Every Israeli soldier carries within him the remembrance of the six million Jews extinguished by the Nazis. A secure State of Israel is the only protection against the repeat of such disaster. This is a notion deeply rooted in every Israeli citizen. The IDF is perceived as being the only force to guarantee that security. Three years of service in the IDF is mandatory for virtually every male and for about 60 percent of the females, when they reach the age of eighteen.[36] Serving in the IDF is a well-established norm in Israeli society. In fact, in no other Western country is there such a long period of universal compulsory military service.

A small number of the best and brightest of these recruits will volunteer to become officers. But only 50 percent of those who volunteer will actually make it through the demanding training it takes to meet the high standards required of officers in the IDF. The nature of the Israeli combat officer has developed into a national institution.[37] Their actions, heroics, and cool leadership under the greatest adversities have been the decisive factor leading to Israel's victories in all its wars. Yet, how the IDF chooses its officers is just as important as their performance in combat.

In the IDF, rank is not a privilege belonging to the right class, but a right earned by ones self-worth. In Syria, for example, only those faithful to the official government party line can become commissioned officers. Commanders are chosen for their loyalty and Bath Party membership rather than their merit as a leader. In the IDF, however, it does not matter whom you voted for, what your social standing is, or where your parents came from. All that matters is that you are among the best in your unit, and each soldier is judged from day one of his military service. Israel has no national military academies, like West Point in the United States or Sandhurst in the United Kingdom, and there are no reserve officer training programs (ROTC) on university campuses. All Israeli officers, with the exception of pilots and naval ship commanders, begin their career of military duty as "lowly" privates.

During the summer, after graduating from secondary school, virtually every eighteen-year-old male reports to basic training. After three-to-five months of basic training in their respective branch of service, recruits are assigned to their designated units for operational service. From day one of his military service, the soldier's skills and qualities as a leader are under observation by his NCOs and officers. The unit commander ranks every new soldier in his unit after observing his performance during training and on operational missions for five months. Every soldier is graded on his personal characteristics, performance, and potential to lead men in combat. The best of the new group of privates is sent to the squad leader's course where he earns the rank of sergeant and becomes an NCO. The squad leader's course is a field oriented learning environment where the young Israeli soldiers are challenged both physically and mentally. With a drop out rate that averages around sixty percent this is the most demanding of all the IDF courses.[38]

Although the squad leader's course is the first rung in the ladder of command, its successful completion does not guarantee anything. The newly promoted sergeant is reassigned to his old unit, where he will serve as squad leader or tank commander.

During the next ten months, his performance during training exercises and real world operational missions will be observed and evaluated. With about one year remaining in the soldier's mandatory three years of national service, he will be considered for the officer course. Only those NCOs with the highest ratings, peer reviews, recommendations by commanding officers, and psychological evaluations are even considered. Positive traits for acceptance into the officer's course are: *sociability, intelligence, emotional stability, leadership capabilities, devotion to one's unit, duty, decisiveness, innovation,* and most importantly, *perseverance under stress and fire*.[39] A soldier who cannot handle himself under fire will not be able to raise his hand as an officer and shout, "follow me" in combat.

Israeli officer candidates undergo essentially the same kind of experiences and training found in most officer training programs as their Western counterparts: field maneuvers, map navigation, weapons systems training, and tactics at the platoon and company levels. However, unlike the typical junior Western military officer, the Israeli counterpart already has two years of experience as a regular soldier and NCO prior to becoming an officer. This allows the IDF to place the emphasis of training on cultivating the officer's ability to solve problems and implement solutions, rather than on learning basic combat skills as the Western officer training must.[40]

Becoming an officer in the IDF is considered an extremely hard-won accomplishment. Only the very best recruits are picked to become NCOs and only about forty percent of those chosen actually achieve that rank. Then only the very best NCOs are picked to attend the officer course and only 50 percent of these make the cut.

The IDF officer is thus commissioned after about twenty-four months of military service and is generally returned to the same unit, where he served as a regular soldier and NCO, to become a platoon leader. Unlike lieutenants in many Western militaries, the young Israeli lieutenant is not "taken under the wing" of his platoon sergeant; rather, the opposite occurs. He is the one who will tutor and supervise his NCOs.[41] The lieutenant's ability to do this stems from two simple facts: first, he has been initially selected because he was the best of the best; and second, he has undergone an intensive program that turns the best soldiers into the best commanders.

Unlike Western counterparts, the IDF has always believed that leading men in combat has more to do with natural talent and "guts" than with an officer's education level. In 1984 the IDF conducted an experiment in which graduates of the academic reserve program were assigned to platoon leader positions with no relationship to their academic specialties. Although these young lieutenants had already demonstrated a higher intellectual level than most of their counterparts, they failed in most cases to translate their intellectual superiority into effective leadership. The IDF concluded that the ability to lead combat units effectively required something more than, or perhaps different from, academic prowess.[42] Congruently, years of combat experience had already proven--an educated man does not necessarily equal a leader of men in combat.

---

[1]U.S. Army, Field Manual 3-0, *Operations* (Fort Monroe: U.S. Army Training and Doctrine Command, 2001), 2-9.

[2]Ibid., 2-11.

[3]James Charlton, ed., *The Military Quotation Book* (New York: St. Martin's Press, 1990), 141.

⁴U.S. Army, Field Manual 22-10, *Army Leadership* (Fort Monroe: U.S. Army Training and Doctrine Command, 1999), 1-1.

⁵Martin Blumenson, *The Patton Papers, 1940-1945* (Boston: Houghton Mifflin Company, 1974), 519.

⁶U.S. Army, Field Manual 22-102: *Soldier Team Development* (Fort Monroe: U.S. Army Training and Doctrine Command, 1987), 54.

⁷Reuven Gal, *A Portrait of the Israeli Soldier* (New York: Greenwood Press, 1986), 7.

⁸George W. Gawrych, *The Albatross of Decisive Victory: War and Policy Between Egypt and Israel in the 1967 and 1973 Arab-Israeli Wars* (Westport, Connecticut: Greenwood Press, 2000), 24.

⁹Israeli Defense Force homepage, available from http://www.idf.il/english/doctrine.stm; Internet.

¹⁰Gal, *A Portrait of the Israeli Soldier*, 10.

¹¹Ibid., 13.

¹²David L. Bongard, "Orde Charles Wingate," in *The Harper Encyclopedia of Military Biography*, 1st ed.

¹³Gal, *A Portrait of the Israeli Soldier*, 7.

¹⁴Yigal Allon, *The Making of Israel's Army* (New York: Universe Books, 1970), 11-12; and Gal, *A Portrait of the Israeli Soldier*, 5.

¹⁵Gal, *A Portrait of the Israeli Soldier*, 120.

¹⁶Avigdor Kahalani, *The Heights of Courage: A Tank Leader's War on the Golan* (New York: Praeger, 1992), 137.

¹⁷Martin Blumenson, *The Patton Papers 1885-1940* (Boston: Houghton Mifflin Company, 1972), 812.

¹⁸Gal, *A Portrait of the Israeli Soldier*, 103.

¹⁹Kahalani, *The Heights of Courage*, 164.

²⁰Samuel Rolbant, *The Israeli Soldier: Profile of an Army* (New York: A. S. Barnes and Company, 1970), 168.

[21]Ze'ev Schiff, *A History of The Israeli Army: 1874 to the Present* (New York: Macmillan Publishing Company, 1985), 228.

[22]Lieutenant Colonel Eytan Yitshak, "Leadership in the Israeli Defense Force," interviewed by Major Oakland McCulloch, Fort Leavenworth, KS, 7 May 2002.

[23]Raful Eitan, *A Soldier's Story: The Life and Times of an Israeli War Hero* (New York: Shapolsky Publishers, 1991), 152.

[24]Schiff, *A History of The Israeli Army*, 118.

[25]S. L. A. Marshall, *Men Against Fire: The Problems of Battle Command in Future War* (New York: William and Morrow, 1947), 48.

[26]Gunther E. Rothenberg, *The Anatomy of the Israeli Army: The Israeli Defence Force, 1948-78* (New York: Hippocrene Books, 1979), 14; and Gal, *A Portrait of the Israeli Soldier*, 70.

[27]Blumenson, *The Patton Papers, 1940-1945*, 251.

[28]Kahalani, *The Heights of Courage*, 50.

[29]Gal, *A Portrait of the Israeli Soldier*, 92.

[30]Kahalani, *The Heights of Courage*, 138.

[31]Aharon Davidi, "Thoughts On Leadership, Command, And Tactics – An Israeli View," interviewed by Captain Roger Cirillo, Fort Leavenworth, KS, 6 April 1981.

[32]Kahalani, *The Heights of Courage*, 102.

[33]Chaim Herzog, *The Arab-Israeli Wars: War and Peace in the Middle East* (New York: Random House, 1982), 341.

[34]Samuel M. Katz, *Fire & Steel: Israel's 7th Armored Brigade* (New York: Pocket Books, 1996), 156.

[35]Gawrych, *The Albatross of Decisive Victory*, 22.

[36]Gal, *A Portrait of the Israeli Soldier*, 32.

[37]Samuel Katz, *Israel's Army* (Novato, California: Presidio Press, 1990), 115.

[38]Gal, *A Portrait of the Israeli Soldier*, 117.

[39]Ibid., 119.

[40]Katz, *Israel's Army*, 118.

[41]Gal, *A Portrait of the Israeli Soldier*, 120.

[42]Ibid., 35.

CHAPTER 4

CONCLUSION

I have conclusively proven that Israeli small-unit leadership was the decisive factor in the Battle for the Golan Heights during the Yom Kippur War in 1973. Despite what appeared to be insurmountable odds, the Israelis determinedly remained in their positions and engaged the advancing masses of Syrian vehicles during four straight days of brutal combat. Just when a Syrian penetration of the defense seemed imminent, the timely commitment of reserve forces would quickly close the gap. These numerous bold counterattacks stole the initiative from the numerically superior Syrian forces, eventually pushing them back across the Purple Line. On several occasions, daring exploits by brave Israeli small-unit leaders completely changed the course of the battle. Furthermore, the absolute fearlessness of the Israeli tank commanders rallied the soldiers and prevented panic, even when death or defeat was looming. The leaders' continually displayed heroism that convinced the soldiers they would accomplish the mission regardless of the situation, virtually ensuring eventual victory.

Obviously, other factors played a role in the Syrian defeat; however, none was as prominent or decisive as Israeli leadership. Occasionally when a battle hangs in the balance, an individual tips the scales toward victory. History provides numerous instances--Desaix at Morengo, Macdonnell at Haugoumont, and Chamberlain on Little Round Top. In the case of the Golan Heights in 1973 it was not an individual that tipped the scales toward victory for the Israelis', but a group of individuals, the Israeli small-unit leaders. While the great numbers of the attacking Syrian force came close to overwhelming the Israeli defenses, it was the great courage and conviction of the Israeli tank commanders that turned the tide of the battle. With such profound determination, a significantly outnumbered Israeli force completely destroyed a massive, modern, Soviet-style Syrian Army on the Golan Heights in 1973.

Relevance to the U.S. Army

The relevance of the Israeli lessons on the Golan Heights during the 1973 Yom Kippur War to the U.S. Army today should be obvious. As the armies of the Western societies continue to get smaller they still face the threat of fighting the massive Soviet-style armies of the "Axis of Evil" for decades to come. Because we will most likely fight outnumbered on future battlefields it is imperative that the U.S. Army produce small-unit leaders who are capable of leading their soldiers to victory, even against insurmountable odds. I have shown how the IDF selects and trains its leaders to ensure that the Israeli Army is ready to meet that type of challenge. I am not suggesting that the U.S. Army adopt the IDF system; however I do believe the U.S. Army must take a hard look at how it selects and trains its small-unit leaders to ensure that they are prepared to fight and win, even if outnumbered on today's modern battlefield.

Let us first look at the commissioning process. In the U.S. Army, officers are not grown and developed through a real selection process like they are in the IDF. The ROTC programs in our universities have been turned into officer recruiting stations where the number of cadets commissioned is more important than the quality of education or training they receive. In a conversation with a current professor of military science I was told,

> The last few years things have become much more "mission" focused. Cadet Command says that they do not sacrifice quality for quantity but I disagree. Every focus is on making numbers and no one ever talks about the quality of education or performance.[1]

Comments such as this were not isolated to a conversation with one PMS; in fact six of the nine PMS's I interviewed made similar comments. There is no real selection process where the best soldiers are chosen to be officers because of their proven leadership skills. Instead we recruit whoever wishes to join a ROTC program, give them a four-year education where very little emphasis is placed on military leadership training and believe we have produced an officer ready to lead men into combat. This is in direct conflict with the 1984 IDF study which concluded that the ability to lead combat units effectively requires something more than, or perhaps different from, academic prowess.

Next, we need to look at how the U.S. Army is training and promoting its officers. On today's modern battlefield, events are occurring at a much faster pace than ever before. On this modern battlefield, leaders must make decisions quickly, and according to the 2001 edition of the U.S. Army's Field Manual 3-0, *Operations*, these decisions are based on the leader's skilled judgment gained from practice, reflection, study, experience and intuition.[2] In the IDF, this practice, experience, and intuition are gained by allowing officers to remain in positions of leadership where these skills are developed through training and operational experience. The problem in the U.S. Army is that officers do not spend enough time in leadership positions to fully develop these valuable skills. In the combat units of the U.S. Army today many lieutenants are lucky to spend a year as a platoon leader where they learn the basics of their new profession; most captains only spend twelve-to-eighteen months in company command; and majors only spend between twelve and eighteen months, on average, as operations officers or executive officers. So by the time an officer in the combat arms is ready to take command of a battalion, after eighteen years of service, he has only been in a position of leadership between three or four years. This is just not enough time for our small-unit leaders to develop the skills that proved so valuable for the IDF on the Golan Heights in 1973.

The last area of concern that must be looked at in the U.S. Army is the Officer Education System (OES). In the IDF every course, from basic training to the squad leader's course to the officer course, are tactically oriented. These courses are designed to produce tactically proficient soldiers and leaders who are able to lead men into combat. This is not the case in the U.S. Army. In a time when the United States Army is placing so much importance on tactical leadership it is shortening the amount of time officers spend at the advanced course and it is placing less emphasis on the tactical level of war at our Command and General Staff College. If the United States Army does not emphasize tactics at these two courses then where? Israeli small-unit leaders were able to make decisions that changed the course of the battle for the Golan Heights because their education ensured that they were tactically proficient. General George S. Patton Jr. said it best when he said, "Good tactics can save even the worst strategy, but bad tactics can ruin even the best strategy."[3] The U.S. Army needs to ensure that it trains its small-unit leaders to be tactically proficient enough that they can save even the worst strategy.

Final Thought

Israel was able to win a decisive victory on the Golan Heights in 1973 because the IDF produced small-unit leaders who led their soldiers to victory. As the former head of the Israeli armored force MG Israel Tal said, "Israel exists by the grace of her dead and living heroes."[4] Many of those heroes are small-unit leaders who gave their lives defending the Golan Heights in 1973, and it was this small-unit leadership that was the decisive factor in the IDFs victory.

---

[1]A Current PMS, interview by MAJ Oakland McCulloch, e-mail conversation, Fort Leavenworth, KS, 4 March 2003

[2]U.S. Army, Field Manual 3-0, *Operations* (Fort Monroe: U.S. Army Training and Doctrine Command, 2001), 5-1.

[3]Martin Blumenson, *The Patton Papers, 1940-1945* (Boston: Houghton Mifflin Company, 1974), 189.

[4]Avigdor Kahalani, *The Heights of Courage: A Tank Leader's War on the Golan* (New York: Praeger, 1992), xiii.

APPENDIX A

ISRAELI BATTLE UNITS AND COMMANDERS

Northern Command Major General Yitzhak Hofi
   Corps Artillery Brigadier General A. Bar-David
   317th Parachute Brigade Colonel Chaim Nadel
   50th Parachute Battalion Lieutenant Colonel Yair Yaron
   18th Parachute Battalion Lieutenant Colonel "Ilan"
   7th Armored Infantry Battalion Lieutenant Colonel Yoav Vaspe
   Northern Command Tank Battalion Lieutenant Colonel Uzi More
   Armor School Tank Battalion Lieutenant Colonel Menahem Ratess

36th Armored Infantry Division Brigadier General Raful Eitan
   188th "Barak" Armored Brigade Colonel Yitzhak Ben-Shoham
   74th Armored Battalion Lieutenant Colonel Yair Nofshe
   53rd Armored Battalion Lieutenant Colonel Oded Eres
   7th Armored Brigade Colonel Avigdor Ben-Gal
   77th Armored Battalion Lieutenant Colonel Avigdor Kahalani
   82nd Armored Battalion Lieutenant Colonel Haim Barak
   75th Armored Infantry Battalion Lieutenant Colonel Yossi Eldar
   1st "Golani" Infantry Brigade Colonel Amir Drori

240th Armored Division Major General Dan Laner
   679th Armored Brigade Colonel Uri Orr
   4th Armored Infantry Brigade Colonel Yaacov Pfeiffer

146th Armored Division Brigadier General Moshe Peled
   9th Armored Infantry Brigade Colonel Mordechai Ben-Porat
   205th Armored Brigade Colonel Yosef Peled
   District Brigade Colonel Zvi Bar
   70th Armored Infantry Brigade Colonel Gideon Gordon

Note 1: The above divisional organizations changed radically during the course of battle. Most notably, *188th Armored Brigade* reverted from its parent *36th Division* to the newly created *240th Division*. Numerous ad hoc units, such as Sarig Force, are not listed here. As divisional sectors were created and as divisional boundaries shifted, brigades and battalions--and parts of brigades and battalions--fell under new commands.

Note 2: Throughout this paper Israeli units will be written in *italicized print* while Syrian units will be written in normal print.

APPENDIX B.

SYRIAN BATTLE UNITS AND COMMANDERS

1st Armored Division Colonel Tewfiq Jehani
    4th Armored Brigade
    91st Armored Brigade
    2nd Mechanized Brigade
    64th Artillery Brigade

3rd Armored Division Brigadier General Mustapha Sharba
    20th Armored Brigade
    65th Armored Brigade
    15th Mechanized Brigade
    13th Artillery Brigade

5th Infantry Division Brigadier General Ali Aslan
    112th Infantry Brigade
    61st Infantry Brigade
    132nd Mechanized Brigade
    50th Artillery Brigade
    47th Independent Armored Brigade (attached)

7th Infantry Division Brigadier General Omar Abrash
    68th Infantry Brigade
    85th Infantry Brigade
    121st Mechanized Brigade
    70th Artillery Brigade
    78th Independent Armored Brigade (attached)

9th Infantry Division Colonel Hassan Tourkmani
    52nd Infantry Brigade
    53rd Infantry Brigade
    43rd Mechanized Brigade
    89th Artillery Brigade
    51st Independent Armored Brigade (attached)

General Headquarters Forces Major General Yousef Chakour
    70th Armored Brigade
    141st Armored Brigade   1st Commando Group
    81st Armored Brigade   82nd Parachute Regiment
    62nd Mechanized Infantry Brigade   Additional Artillery Brigades
    30th Infantry Brigade
    69th Rocket Brigade
    90th Infantry Brigade

APPENDIX C

ILLUSTRATIONS

Map of the Golan Heights with the Relief of the Golan Heights

Map of Key Locations on the Golan Heights

Map of the Golan Heights Deployments on 6 October 1973 at 1400 Hours

Map of the Deployment of Forces on 7 October 1973 at 1400 Hours

Map of the Maximum Syrian Penetration on 7 October 1973 at 2400 Hours

Map of Israeli Counterattacks Reaching the Purple Line on 10 October 1973

Figure 1. Map of the Golan Heights with the Relief of the Golan Heights

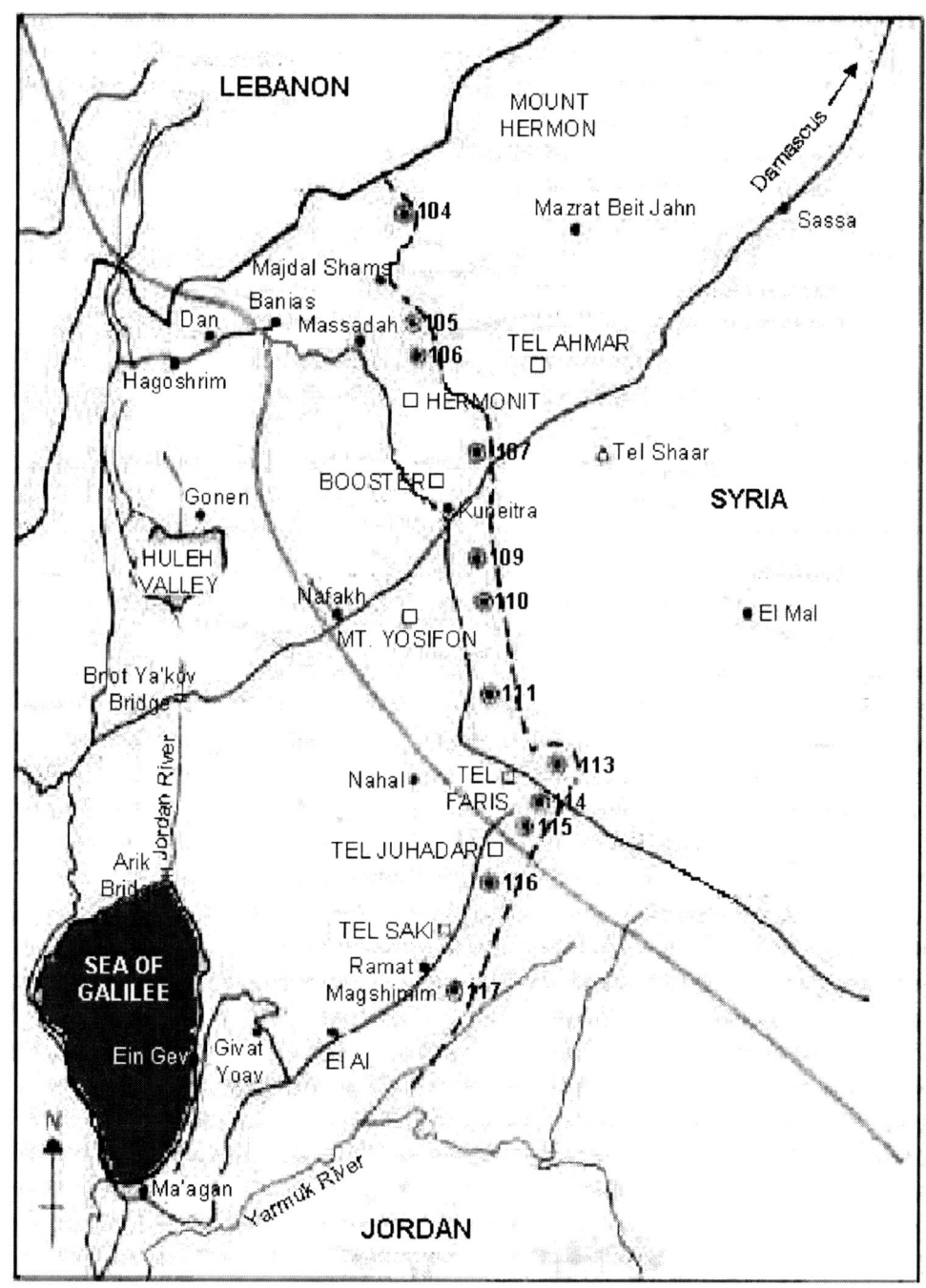

Figure 2. Map of Key Locations on the Golan Heights

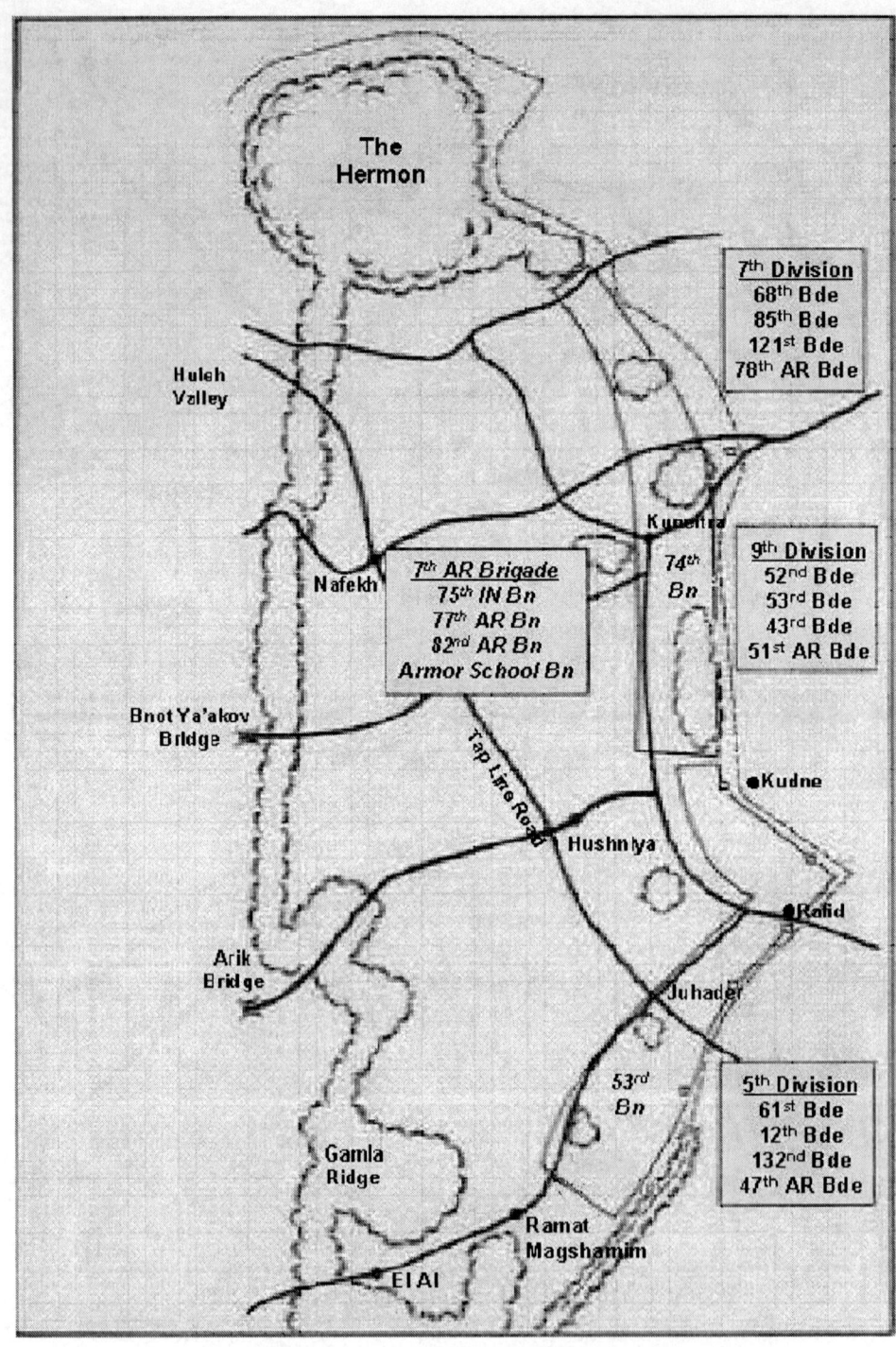

Figure 3. The Golan Heights Deployment, 6 October 1973 at 1400 Hours

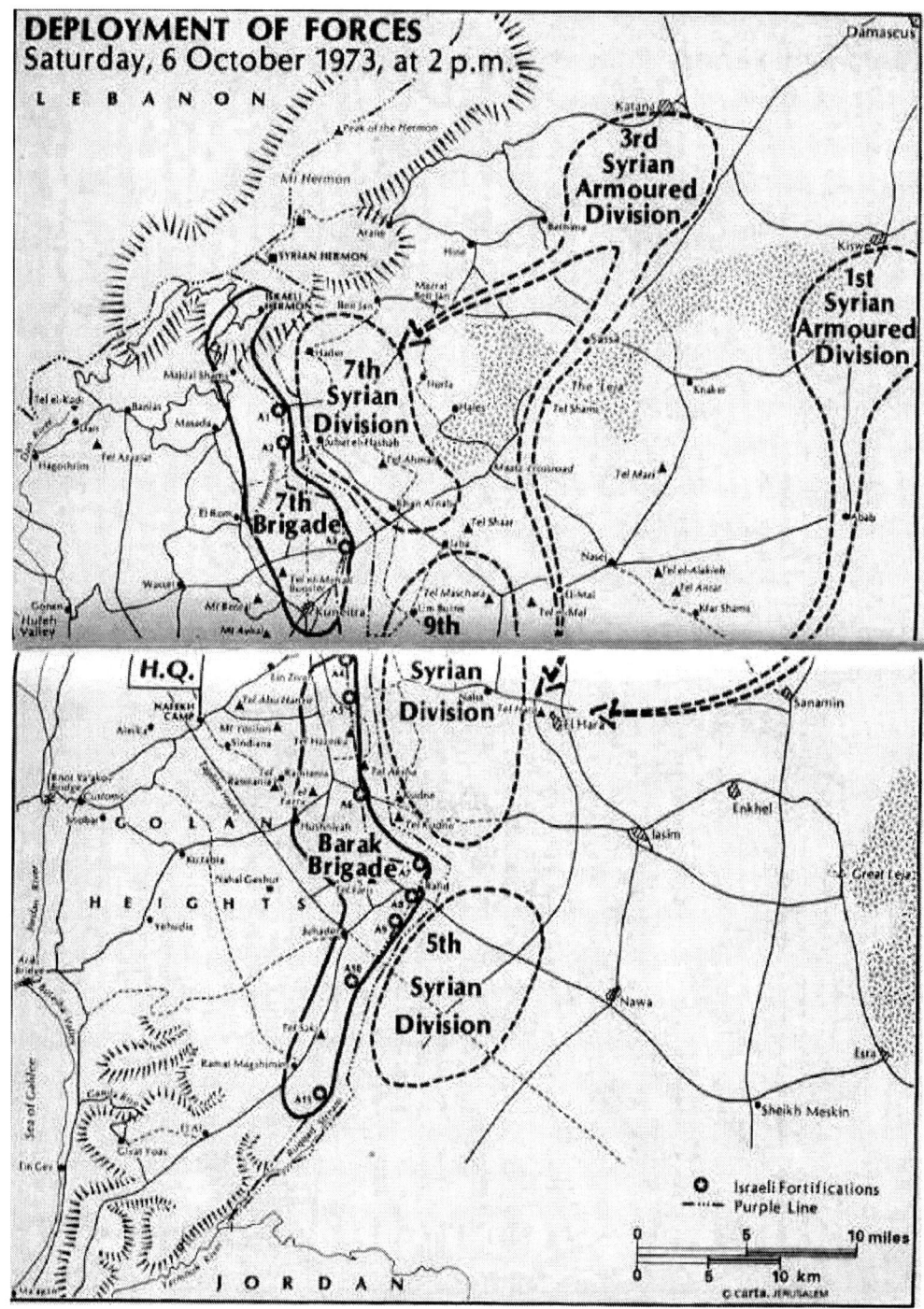

Figure 4. Deployment of Forces, Saturday, 6 October 1943, at 2 p.m.

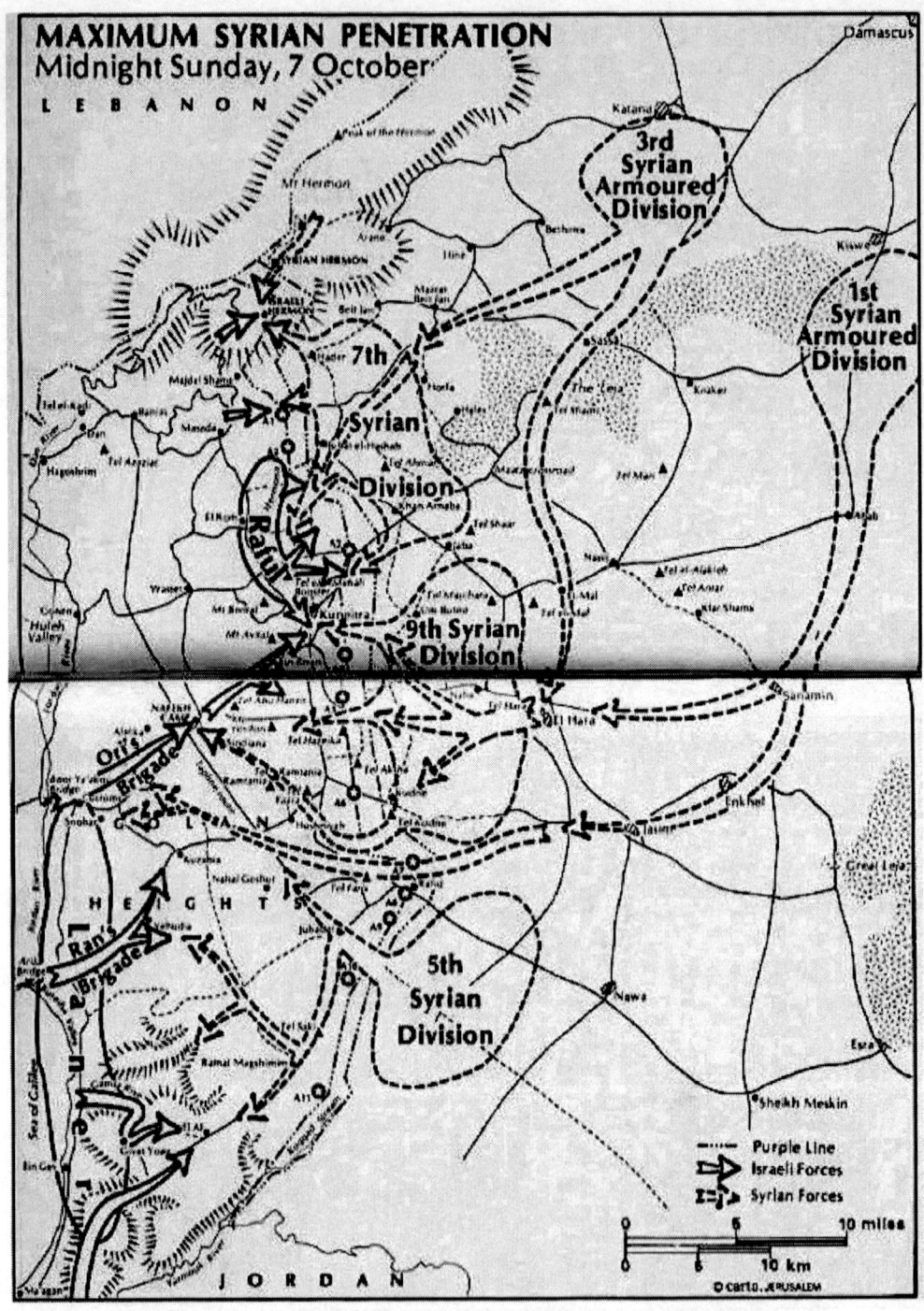

Figure 5. Maximum Syrian Penetration Midnight, Sunday, 7 October

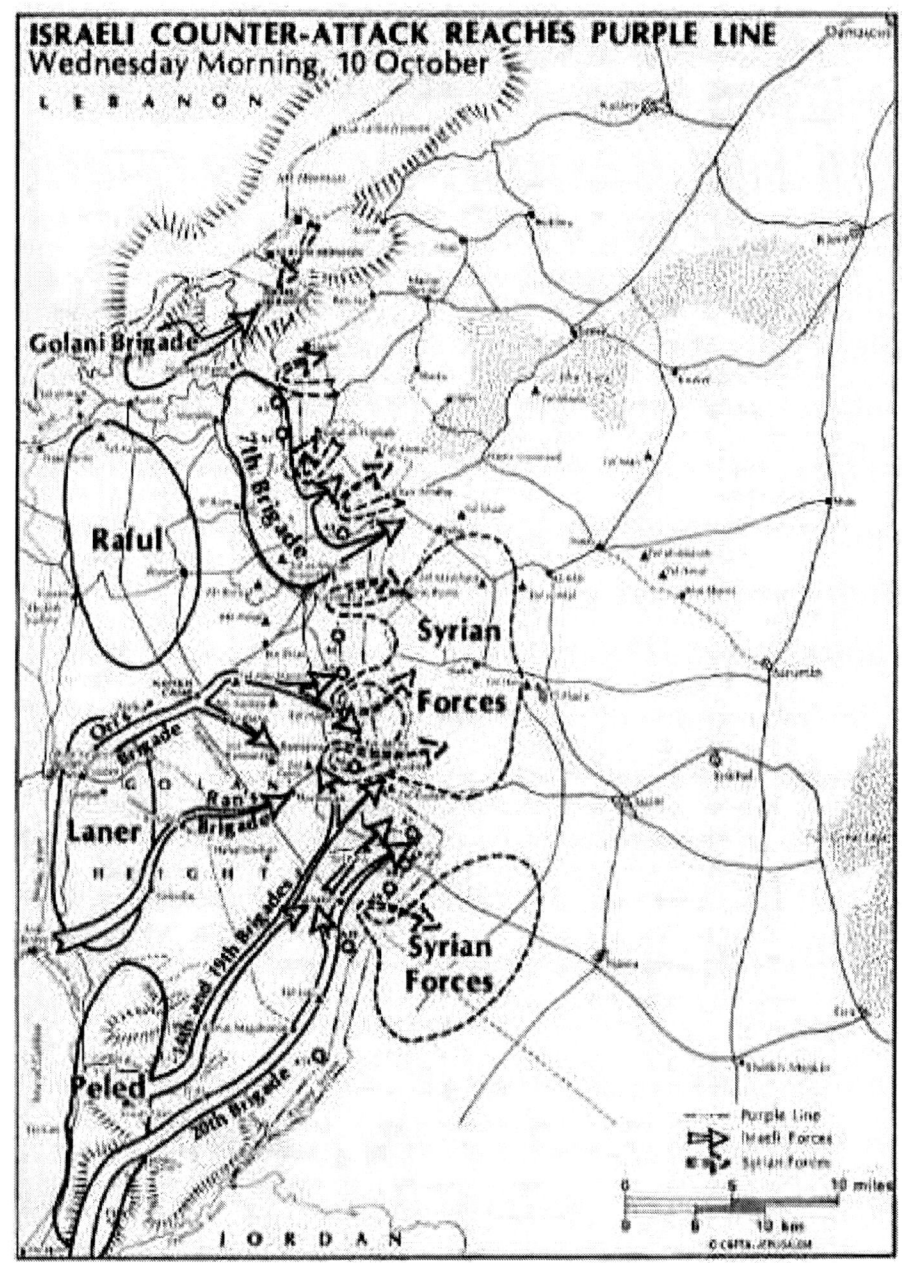

Figure 6. Israeli Counterattack Reaches Purple Line

APPENDIX D

ISRAELI OFFICER'S OATH OF OFFICE

"I hereby swear, and fully commit myself, to be faithful to the State of Israel, to its constitution and its authorities, to take upon myself, without reservation or hesitancy, the rules of discipline of the Israeli Defense Force, to obey all commands and orders given by authorized commanders, and to devote all my strength, and even sacrifice my life, to the defense of my country and the freedom of Israel."

APPENDIX E

ISRAELI AND SYRIAN TANK AND ARMORED FIGHTING VEHICLE SPECIFICATIONS

Centurion Main Battle Tank Identification Features
- **Supported track**
- **6 road wheels with gap between the 2nd and 3rd**
- **3 piece side skirt exposing last road wheel and sprocket**
- **Stowage boxes and mufflers mounted on fenders**
- **Driver located front right of hull with 2 piece hatch**
- **Cast turret with commander and gunner on right and loader on the left**
- **Large stowage bin on the right side of turret with 2 smaller bins on the left separated by a pistol port**
- **Large rectangular gun mantlet**
- **105-mm gun with bore evacuator located 2/3rds back from the muzzle**

Specifications

Crew	Armament	Ammunition	Length	Width	Height	Weight	Engine	Max Road Speed	Gradient
4	105-mm main gun 7.62-mm coaxial machine gun 7.62-mm antiaircraft machine gun 12.7-mm RMG 2 x 6 smoke dischargers	64 x 105 mm 600 x 12.7 mm 4.750 x 7.62mm	7.823 m	3.39 m	3.009 m	51,820 kg	Rolls-Royce Mk IVB 12-cylinder liquid-cooled petrol developing 650 bhp at 2,550 rpm	34.6 kph	60%
Side Slope	Fuel Capacity	Max Range	Fording	Vertical Obstacle	Trench	Armor	NBC System	Night Vision Equipment	
40%	1037 lit	190 km	1.45 m	0.914 m	3.352 m	Steel (152 mm)	No	No	

Manufacturer: Vickers, Leyland Motors, Royal Ordnance Leeds, and Royal Ordnance Woolwich

BMP-1 INFANTRY FIGHTING VEHICLE
Specifications

Crew	3 + 8
Armament	73-mm cannon 1 x 7.62-mm machine gun SAGGER ATGW launcher
Ammunition	40 x 73 mm 2,000 x 7.62 mm 1+4 SAGGER ATGW
Length	6.74 m
Width	2.94 m
Height	2.15 m
Weight	13,500 kg
Engine	Type UTD-20 6-cylinder in line-water-cooled diesel developing 300 hp at 2,000 rpm
Max Road Speed	80 kmh
Gradient	60%
Side Slope	30%
Fuel Capacity	460 lit
Max Range	500 km
Fording	Amphibious
Vertical Obstacle	0.8 m
Trench	2.2 m
Armor	Steel (33 mm)
NBC System	Yes
Night Vision Equipment	Yes (infrared)

Manufacturer: Czechoslovak and former Soviet state arsenals

T-55 Main Battle Tank Specifications	
Crew	4
Armament	100-mm main gun 7.62-mm coaxial machine gun 7.62-mm machine gun (bow) 12.7-mm AA MG
Ammunition	34 x 100 mm 500 x 12.7 mm 3,000 x 7.62 mm
Length	6.45 m
Width	3.27 m
Height	2.4 m
Weight	36,000 kg
Engine	V-12 water-cooled diesel- developing 520 hp at 2,000 rpm
Max Road Speed	48 kph
Gradient	60%
Side Slope	40%
Fuel Capacity	812 lit
Max Range	400 km - 600 km with aux tanks
Fording	1.4 m 4.5 m w/prep
Vertical Obstacle	0.8 m
Trench	2.7 m
Armor	Steel - 203 mm max
NBC System	No
Night Vision Equipment	Yes - infrared

Manufacturer: Czechoslovakian, Poland, former Soviet State Factories, and China as Type 59

T-62 Main Battle Tank
Specifications

Crew	4
Armament	115-mm main gun 7.6-2-mm coaxial machine gun 12.7-mm AA MG smoke dischargers (number depends on model)
Ammunition	40 x 115 mm 300 x 12.7 mm 2,500 x 7.62 mm
Length	6.63 m
Width	3.3 m
Height	2.395 m
Weight	40,000 kg
Engine	V-55-5 V-12 diesel 580 hp at 2,000 rpm
Max Road Speed	50 kph
Gradient	60%
Side Slope	30%
Fuel Capacity	675 lit + 285 lit (aux)
Max Range	450 km-650 km with aux tanks
Fording	1.4 m 5 m w/prep
Vertical Obstacle	0.8 m
Trench	2.85 m
Armor	Steel - 242 mm max
NBC System	Yes
Night Vision Equipment	Yes - infrared

Manufacturer: Czechoslovakian, North Korean, and former Soviet State Factories

BIBLIOGRAPHY

Books

Adan, Avraham. *On The Banks of the Suez.* Presidio: Presidio Press, 1980.

Allon, Yigal. *The Making of Israel's Army.* New York: Universe Books, 1970.

Asher, Jerry, and Eric Hammel. *Duel For The Golan: The 100-Hour Battle That Saved Israel.* New York: William Morrow and Company, 1987.

Blumenson, Martin. *The Patton Papers, 1885-1940.* Boston: Houghton Mifflin Company, 1974.

_____. *The Patton Papers, 1940-1945.* Boston: Houghton Mifflin Company, 1972.

Charlton, James, ed. *The Military Quotation Book.* New York: St. Martin's Press, 1990.

Dupuy, Trevor N. *Elusive Victory: The Arab-Israeli Wars, 1947-1974.* Fairfax: Hero Books, 1984.

Eitan, Raful. *A Soldier's Story: The Life and Times of an Israeli War Hero.* New York: Shapolsky Publishers, 1991.

Eshel, David. *Chariots of the Desert: The Story of the Israeli Armoured Corps.* London: Brassey's Defence Publishers, 1989.

Gal, Reuven. *A Portrait of the Israeli Soldier.* New York: Greenwood Press, 1986.

Gawrych, George W. *The Albatross of Decisive Victory: War and Policy Between Egypt and Israel in the 1967 and 1973 Arab-Israeli Wars.* Westport: Greenwood Press, 2000.

Herzog, Chaim. *The Arab-Israeli Wars: War and Peace in the Middle East.* New York: Random House, 1982.

_____. *The War of Atonement.* Boston: Little, Brown and Company, 1975.

Kahalani, Avigdor. *The Heights of Courage: A Tank Leader's War on the Golan.* London: Greenwood Press, 1984.

Katz, Samuel M. *Israeli Tank Battles: Yom Kippur to Lebanon.* London: Arms and Armor Press, 1988.

_____. *Fire & Steel: Israel's 7th Armored Brigade.* New York: Pocket Books, 1996.

_____. *Israel's Army.* Novato: Presidio Press, 1990.

Marshall, S.L.A. *Men Against Fire: The Problems of Battle Command in Future War.* New York: William and Morrow, 1947.

Pollack, Kenneth M. *Arabs At War: Military Effectiveness, 1948-1991.* Lincoln: University of Nebraska Press, 2002.

Rolbant, Samuel. *The Israeli Soldier: Profile of an Army.* New York: A.S. Barnes and Company, 1970.

Rothenberg, Gunther E. *The Anatomy of the Israeli Army: The Israeli Defence Force, 1948-78.* New York: Hippocrene Books, 1978.

Schiff, Ze'ev. *A History of The Israeli Army: 1874 to the Present.* New York: Macmillan Publishing, 1985.

Van Crevald, Martin. *The Sword and the Olive: A Critical History of the Israeli Defense Force.* New York: Public Affairs, 1998.

Periodicals

Rashba, Gary. "Sacrificial Stand in the Golan Heights." *Military History Magazine*, 1 October 1998, 3.

Weller, Jac. "Middle East Tank Killers." *Royal United Services Institute Journal*, December 1974: 12.

Government Documents

U.S. Army, Field Manual 3-0, *Operations.* Fort Monroe, VA: U.S. Army Training and Doctrine Command, June 2001.

U.S. Army, Field Manual 22-100, *Army Leadership.* Fort Monroe, VA: U.S. Army Training and Doctrine Command, August 1999.

U.S. Army, Field Manual 22-102, *Soldier Team Development.* Fort Monroe, VA: U.S. Army Training and Doctrine Command, July 1987.

Other Sources

Bongard, David L., "Orde Charles Wingate." In *The Harper Encyclopedia of Military Biography*, 1st ed.

Davidi, Aharon. "Thoughts On Leadership, Command, And Tactics – An Israeli View." Interviewed by CPT Roger Cirillo (Combat Studies Institute, Command and General Staff College, Fort Leavenworth, KS., 6 April 1981).

Israeli Defense Force. 2003. *Israeli Military Doctrine.* Database on-line. Available at http://www.idf.il/english/doctrine.stm

Trautman, Robin. 2003. *The Yom Kippur War.* The Jewish Student Online Research Center. Database on-line. Available from North Park University, http://campus.northpark.edu/history/WebChron/MiddleEast/YomKippurWar.html

Yitshak, Eytan, Lieutenant Colonel Israeli Army. Interview by author, 7 May 2002, Fort Leavenworth. Tape recording. Command and General Staff College, Fort Leavenworth, KS.

INITIAL DISTRIBUTION LIST

Combined Arms Research Library
U.S. Army Command and General Staff College
250 Gibbon Ave.
Fort Leavenworth, KS 66027-1352

Defense Technical Information Center/OCA
825 John J. Kingman Rd., Suite 944
Fort Belvoir, VA 22060-6218

Dr. George W. Gawrych
CSI
USACGSC
1 Reynolds Ave.
Fort Leavenworth, KS 66027-1352

COL Lawyn C. Edwards
CSI
USACGSC
1 Reynolds Ave.
Fort Leavenworth, KS 66027-1352

LTC William L. Greenberg
CTAC
USACGSC
1 Reynolds Ave.
Fort Leavenworth, KS 66027-1352

CERTIFICATION FOR MMAS DISTRIBUTION STATEMENT

1. Certification Date: 6 June 2003

2. Thesis Author: MAJ Oakland McCulloch

3. Thesis Title: The Decisiveness of Israeli Small-Unit Leadership on the Golan Heights in the 1973 Yom Kippur War

4. Thesis Committee Members: _____

   Signatures: _____

   _____

5. Distribution Statement: See distribution statements A-X on reverse, then circle appropriate distribution statement letter code below:

(A) B C D E F X   SEE EXPLANATION OF CODES ON REVERSE

If your thesis does not fit into any of the above categories or is classified, you must coordinate with the classified section at CARL.

6. Justification: Justification is required for any distribution other than described in Distribution Statement A. All or part of a thesis may justify distribution limitation. See limitation justification statements 1-10 on reverse, then list, below, the statement(s) that applies (apply) to your thesis and corresponding chapters/sections and pages. Follow sample format shown below:

EXAMPLE

Limitation Justification Statement	/	Chapter/Section	/	Page(s)
Direct Military Support (10)	/	Chapter 3	/	12
Critical Technology (3)	/	Section 4	/	31
Administrative Operational Use (7)	/	Chapter 2	/	13-32

Fill in limitation justification for your thesis below:

Limitation Justification Statement	/	Chapter/Section	/	Page(s)
_____	/	_____	/	_____
_____	/	_____	/	_____
_____	/	_____	/	_____
_____	/	_____	/	_____
_____	/	_____	/	_____

7. MMAS Thesis Author's Signature: _____

STATEMENT A: Approved for public release; distribution is unlimited. (Documents with this statement may be made available or sold to the general public and foreign nationals).

STATEMENT B: Distribution authorized to U.S. Government agencies only (insert reason and date ON REVERSE OF THIS FORM). Currently used reasons for imposing this statement include the following:

    1. Foreign Government Information. Protection of foreign information.

    2. Proprietary Information. Protection of proprietary information not owned by the U.S. Government.

    3. Critical Technology. Protection and control of critical technology including technical data with potential military application.

    4. Test and Evaluation. Protection of test and evaluation of commercial production or military hardware.

    5. Contractor Performance Evaluation. Protection of information involving contractor performance evaluation.

    6. Premature Dissemination. Protection of information involving systems or hardware from premature dissemination.

    7. Administrative/Operational Use. Protection of information restricted to official use or for administrative or operational purposes.

    8. Software Documentation. Protection of software documentation - release only in accordance with the provisions of DoD Instruction 7930.2.

    9. Specific Authority. Protection of information required by a specific authority.

    10. Direct Military Support. To protect export-controlled technical data of such military significance that release for purposes other than direct support of DoD-approved activities may jeopardize a U.S. military advantage.

STATEMENT C: Distribution authorized to U.S. Government agencies and their contractors: (REASON AND DATE). Currently most used reasons are 1, 3, 7, 8, and 9 above.

STATEMENT D: Distribution authorized to DoD and U.S. DoD contractors only; (REASON AND DATE). Currently most reasons are 1, 3, 7, 8, and 9 above.

STATEMENT E: Distribution authorized to DoD only; (REASON AND DATE). Currently most used reasons are 1, 2, 3, 4, 5, 6, 7, 8, 9, and 10.

STATEMENT F: Further dissemination only as directed by (controlling DoD office and date), or higher DoD authority. Used when the DoD originator determines that information is subject to special dissemination limitation specified by paragraph 4-505, DoD 5200.1-R.

STATEMENT X: Distribution authorized to U.S. Government agencies and private individuals of enterprises eligible to obtain export-controlled technical data in accordance with DoD Directive 5230.25; (date). Controlling DoD office is (insert).

Lightning Source UK Ltd.
Milton Keynes UK
UKOW01f2105220813

215836UK00010B/753/P